Developing attitudes to recognition: substantial differences in an age of globalisation

E. Stephen Hunt and Sjur Bergan (eds)

Council of Europe Publishing

Cover design and layout: Documents and Publications Production Department (SPDP), Council of Europe

Council of Europe Publishing
F-67075 Strasbourg Cedex
http://book.coe.int

ISBN 978-92-871-6697-5
© Council of Europe, December 2009
Printed at the Council of Europe

Contents

Preface

Carita Blomqvist
President of the Lisbon Recognition Convention Committee

I am pleased to write the preface to this new book in the Council of Europe Higher Education Series. The topic of substantial differences is highly important in the implementation of the Council of Europe/UNESCO Convention on the Recognition of Qualifications concerning Higher Education in the European Region. Beyond that, as this book makes clear, our view of education and the qualifications to which education leads, lies behind the term "substantial differences".

The fair recognition of foreign qualifications is essential, not only for establishing a European Higher Education Area, but also for global mobility. The fundamental principle of the convention, usually applied to applicants from all over the world, is that all applicants have the right to a fair assessment of their qualifications within a reasonable time limit, according to transparent, coherent and reliable procedures and without discrimination. Notwithstanding this, the convention makes it possible for the competent recognition authority not to recognise a foreign qualification, or to recognise it only partly, in cases where the authority can demonstrate that there is a substantial difference.

To guarantee equal and fair treatment of applicants, the concept of substantial difference has been explored widely on an institutional, national, European and even on a global level. This book contributes to this discussion in a number of ways, including the presentation of several fictitious case studies, which have been discussed in the ENIC and NARIC networks.[1] As the articles in this book show, it is impossible to define precise features of substantial differences that could be applied to all situations. This book also demonstrates that a discussion about the implementation of the convention and the actual basis for recognition decisions must be continued – how and on what basis do recognition authorities come to the conclusion that a substantial difference exists?

On the other hand, it could be useful to consider the issue from a somewhat different angle: not so much focusing on the substantial difference and whether it exists or not, but rather emphasising the fact that in some cases – depending, for example, on the purpose of recognition – it might be possible to ignore differences and accept

---

1. The Europe Network of National Information Centres on academic recognition and mobility (ENIC Network) is served jointly by the Council of Europe and UNESCO and encompasses all parties to the Lisbon Recognition Convention as well as any countries party to the European Cultural Convention and/or members of the UNESCO Europe Region not yet party to the Lisbon Recognition Convention. The NARIC Network of National Academic Recognition Information Centres is run by the European Commission and encompasses all countries of the European Union and the European Economic Area as well as relevant Commission programmes in higher education. The two networks co-operate closely and hold joint annual meetings.

their existence. This, again, could lead to more favourable recognition decisions. This is where the discussion about developing (or changing) attitudes comes in, and it is not least in this context that this book is important.

Sjur Bergan points out in this book that the recognition of qualifications may also be considered as a public service, since it is carried out with a public mandate. This leads us to good administration, which should also – or should we say especially – be a guiding principle when decisions or recommendations concerning the rights of individuals are made. The principles of good administration may vary to a certain extent, depending on the situation and the geographical region, but nevertheless there exist such commonly accepted principles as transparency, consistency, accountability, responsiveness, effectiveness, efficiency and proportionality. All these principles can and should be followed when making decisions on recognition – some of them are already emphasised by the convention itself, or its subsidiary texts, such as the Recommendation on Criteria and Procedures for the Assessment of Foreign Qualifications and Periods of Study.

In addition to the principles mentioned above, the principle of being service-focused is nowadays often added to the list of qualities for good administration. This means dealing with people sensitively and flexibly and having regard for their individual circumstances – while at the same time being consistent with the recognition deci-sions made previously in similar situations. In an assessment process this might, for example, mean considering positively prior learning obtained outside formal qualifications. Being service-focused could also imply that if there are two valid ways to solve an issue, the one more favourable to the applicant should be selected.

I believe that this book raises awareness of recognition issues, and especially of fair recognition. It provides an interesting collection of case studies, which represent the issues often faced by recognition authorities. I trust that this book will lead to greater insight into the concept of substantial difference, as well as into the process of fair recognition of foreign qualifications.

This book has been edited by E. Stephen Hunt and Sjur Bergan, whom I would like to thank for their consistent and hard work on behalf of fair recognition policies in Europe and beyond – their articles in this book being examples of this work. The writers of individual chapters are close colleagues from different countries and I would like to thank them too for bringing their expertise to a wide audience.

Introduction

Sjur Bergan and E. Stephen Hunt

How, in the age of marketing and sound bites, can one elicit interest in a book on substantial differences? In part, this is an issue of target groups. In the community of credentials evaluators and other specialists on the recognition of qualifications, this seemingly obscure concept needs no further recommendation or advertisement. In spite of its seemingly dry and technical nature, it is as exciting to recognition specialists as black holes are to astrophysicists, integers to mathematicians and aspect or ergativity to linguists.

If we broaden the target group, the case for why somebody should read this book may seem more difficult to make. Nevertheless, we are convinced that the arguments made in this volume are well worth the attention of educational policy makers and all those with a serious interest in education. This is because, in spite of its seemingly high level of technicality, the concept of substantial differences goes to the core of the educational debate. What do learners know and understand and what are they able to do on the basis of a qualification? How can this be expressed and described? And how can learners carry their qualifications across borders without leaving a part of their real value behind? In discussions of substantial differences, the technical meets the philosophical, the administrative meets the political. Decisions on recognition made when considering whether a difference is substantial are based on the future opportunities for study and employment for those who apply, but also say much about how those who make the decisions view themselves, their education system and their societies.

Think of recognition as a bridge that learners have to cross in order to move from one education system to another. Bridges often span accidents of nature, like rivers or valleys, and sometimes they span accidents of the human mind, like administrative borders. In the latter case, those who move across the bridge may need to comply with formalities – which can also be accidents of the human mind – such as customs regulations. Think of qualifications – what learners know, understand and are able to do – as a suitcase or a backpack that has to be carried across the bridge. If the bridge enables learners to cross the divide between two education systems, they may well be faced by a "customs office" at the other end of the bridge, in the shape of regulations and practices for the recognition of their qualifications, and sometimes learners may also feel that these are accidents of the human mind.

This book sets out to look at ways in which the treatment of qualifications that move across borders could be made less "accidental". Everyone would agree that the real value of qualifications should be fairly recognised, and everyone would agree that, in some cases, the differences between two qualifications are too significant for them to be considered as being of equal value.

General agreement on such very broad issues leaves ample scope for consideration of details. Sometimes this consideration will prove that "the devil is in the details" and sometimes an excess of details can make principled arguments difficult.

How we view differences between qualifications can reveal a great deal about our approach to education. How similar does a qualification need to be to the ones given in our own country for the foreign qualification to be of equal value? Does equal value also mean equal use? What if the foreign qualification is clearly of the right level but its focus is different? What if the foreign language learner has an excellent practical and theoretical grasp of a given language, but has less understanding of the country in which the language is spoken, or less knowledge of its literature than one would expect from a graduate in our own country? What if the foreign engineer has adequate training in the theoretical aspects of engineering, but has had no exposure to the specific requirements of countries that, say, are subjected to a lot of snow, or are exposed to earthquakes?

These and many other questions, lead us to this book. They lead us to a consideration of when foreign qualifications should be recognised and when they should not. They lead us to a consideration of substantial differences.

The concept of substantial differences arises from the legal framework for the recognition of qualifications in the European Region, which encompasses geographical Europe as well as North America, parts of Central Asia and Israel and with which Australia and New Zealand are associated, by virtue of being parties to its legal framework for recognition. The basic legal text is the Council of Europe/UNESCO Convention on the Recognition of Qualifications concerning Higher Education in the European Region (ETS No. 165), also known as the Lisbon Recognition Convention or the Council of Europe/UNESCO Recognition Convention, which was adopted in 1997.[2]

The basic principle of this convention is that all applicants should be given fair recognition of their foreign qualifications. Fair recognition implies that the qualifications should be recognised unless the competent authorities can demonstrate that there is a substantial difference between the applicant's qualifications and the similar qualifications of the country in which recognition is sought.

No legal text, however, can give a comprehensive overview of what might constitute substantial differences. This is an understanding that can only be developed through consideration of practice, and that is what the ENIC[3] and NARIC[4] networks have been doing. This book is the result of extensive discussions within the networks in the period 2005-08, when recognition specialists from the 50 or so countries that

---

2. Countries that are not a part of the European Region may accede to the convention, as Australia and New Zealand have done.
3. European Network of Information Centres on academic recognition and mobility, served jointly by the Council of Europe and UNESCO.
4. Network of National Academic Recognition Information Centres, served by the European Commission.

make up the networks attempted to develop a better common understanding of this seemingly elusive concept.

The first part of the book analyses the concept of substantial differences and seeks to put it into context. Sjur Bergan's article is entitled "exploring a concept", and the title serves to underline that our understanding of substantial differences is not set in stone. As our societies evolve, so should our understanding of which differences between qualifications are crucial and which are not. A couple of generations ago, a knowledge of Latin was considered *de rigueur* in many countries for any kind of academic study, but few education systems or institutions take this view today. A knowledge of Latin may be a sign of culture, but it is not a *sine qua non* for gaining access to most study programmes. It may even be worth bearing in mind that while one cannot function in modern societies without being able to read and write, literacy was a highly specialised skill in many societies throughout history and entirely absent from many more. In these societies, it was entirely possible to be educated, according to the standards of the society, without being literate. In our societies, this is of course impossible, and not only traditional literacy but also computer literacy has come to be taken for granted.

Before discussing the details of those things which may or may not be considered to be substantial differences, it is important to understand the reasoning behind the concept. Essentially, substantial differences are those that may have a serious impact on the fitness of the qualification for the purpose for which the learner would like to use it. While this seems fairly straightforward as a principle, Sjur Bergan's article exploring the concept seeks to develop the reasoning behind the concept in some detail and to outline possible issues of debate or disagreement.

The second part of the book is intended to illustrate different aspects of the concept through practical examples. With one exception – Bas Wegewijs' article – the seven articles in this part of the book discuss fictitious cases. This was done in part to avoid participants in the discussions feeling the need to defend their own education system or recognition practice, rather than try to examine cases with an open mind, and in part to enable the writers to construct "ideal cases" that would clearly bring out one or more specific aspects of the concept. Hence, the articles consider differences in the duration of study and the profile of study programmes (the article by Peter J. Wells and Rolf Lofstad), differences in the status of programmes (the articles by E. Stephen Hunt and Yves E. Beaudin) and the particular cases of various regulated professions (the articles by Erwin Malfroy and E. Stephen Hunt). The article by Françoise Profit and Jean-Philippe Restoueix considers another important issue that frequently leads to different interpretations of the concept under discussion: the question of whether different learning paths – some of which may be non-traditional – leading to similar qualifications in different countries could be considered a substantial difference.

All articles in this part of the book are based on cases that were presented to and discussed by members of the ENIC and NARIC networks, and they seek to reflect on the diversity of opinions expressed in the discussion. They also take an analytical approach. The purpose is not to provide a single "correct" answer, because even if there are a good number of incorrect answers, there is rarely only one valid way of looking at a given qualification. The seven case studies are intended to support and illustrate the points of principle made elsewhere in the book and to make the theoretical considerations more easily accessible.

The third part takes a broader view of substantial differences. The article by Bas Wegewijs and Lucie de Bruin reports the findings of a survey on how a number of European information centres considered a set of foreign qualifications. The survey is interesting, not only because it collected a unique sample of reasoned opinions, but also because the survey included a sample of views of what should be considered commendable and less commendable practice. This is important because not all credentials evaluators feel they are free to follow what they themselves consider would be best practice. In some cases, they may be constrained by laws and regulations, while in other cases the established practice of their centres or the expectations of the academic community may be such that it will take quite some time and sustained effort to change current practice. Hopefully this book will help those efforts.

In the other articles in this section, a set of broader issues are considered. Sjur Bergan examines whether it is possible to identify different cultures of recognition, so that one's perception of what constitutes substantial difference is coloured by the culture to which one belongs. It is important to note that "culture" refers not only to national backgrounds and values, but to one's perception of education and one's general attitudes to difference and similarities. He suggests that there are indeed two different "recognition cultures" in the European Region.

E. Stephen Hunt examines a particularly difficult issue: are qualifications from non-recognised institutions by definition "substantially different"? While nearly everyone is familiar with the problem of bogus institutions or "degree mills" and may have dealt with substandard institutions, there are other classes of institution that are legitimate – often high-quality providers that are not recognised due to legal or policy issues not because of their educational worth. Government and military educational institutions, religious seminaries, adult education centres and others often fall outside the jurisdiction of ministries of education, even though their programmes satisfy other recognition criteria and their graduates are eligible for private and even public employment. The case of defunct but previously recognised institutions and programmes, or those that have changed due to educational reforms, are also considered.

In the final article in this section, Sjur Bergan examines the potential role of qualifications frameworks in helping to define substantial differences. While few countries had qualifications frameworks as recently as five years ago, they have now become an essential element of higher education reform in the European Higher Education Area, and many countries outside Europe are also developing frameworks, following the pioneers in the field: Australia, New Zealand and South Africa. Where they exist, qualifications frameworks should be used as an important instrument to facilitate recognition, but they do not provide "automatic recognition", nor should the absence of qualifications frameworks legitimately be considered a substantial difference in its own right. Many countries are still developing theirs and other countries may decide not to have qualifications frameworks.

The fourth and final part of the book seeks to outline the current state of affairs, with respect to recognition and the issue of substantial difference, and to discuss a future agenda. E. Stephen Hunt summarises history and current policy with respect to substantial difference and provides information, derived from research, on good practices and not-so-good practices. Sjur Bergan also looks back to the 1990s, in order to put the future challenges in context and to suggest some ways forward. With the international legal framework in place, the most difficult challenge remains: that of changing attitudes to recognition and developing good practice throughout the European Region. This will require further work at the European Region level, as well as in each country and at each institution.

In one sense, the challenges are unlikely ever to be fully met. As views of the roles and purposes of education evolve, so must recognition practice. Even if perfection is unlikely, real and continued improvement of practice is, however, both possible and necessary. We hope this book, as well as the discussions in the ENIC and NARIC networks, will provide a solid basis for the continuing development of good practice, but that practice will not be developed on the basis of a book alone. The individual ENIC and NARIC centres must play a key role in their respective countries, where they must work with credentials evaluators at higher education institutions, as well as with employers' organisations, policy makers and other stakeholders. The ENIC and NARIC centres must lead the way in their respective countries, in the same way that the networks have led the way at the level of the European Region.

The need to improve recognition practice is not, of course, limited to the European Region. Whatever the terminology used, developing a better common understanding of substantial differences should also be at the top of the recognition agenda worldwide. Through UNESCO's system of regional conventions for Africa, the Arab world, Asia and the Pacific, Latin America and the Caribbean and the Mediterranean, in addition to the European Region, where the Lisbon Recognition Convention is the regional reference, recognition practice could be developed through discussion and working groups involving all or at least several regions. The ENIC and NARIC networks have made a modest start in this direction, by establishing a working group on recognition in the global context. An understanding of why we take the view of educational qualifications that we do, and of why different countries and regions may tend to take one view or the other, is essential to working towards a better common understanding. In this work, it is important that we, from the European Region, keep in mind that while we are right in underlining the need for fair recognition of our own qualifications in other parts of the

11

world, we must also consider qualifications from elsewhere with the same openness of mind with which we would like our own qualifications to be considered.

We hope this book will help clarify concepts and provide useful illustrations to stimulate further debate, but above all that it will help develop better practice and help all those who need to move across borders obtain fair recognition of their qualifications.

I. Concepts and principles

Substantial differences: exploring a concept

Sjur Bergan

Background

The fair recognition of qualifications is a *sine qua non* of international mobility. Fair recognition is, by itself, not sufficient to stimulate mobility but, at the same time, academic mobility is unthinkable as a mass phenomenon without fair recognition. Gone are the days when most students were content with a stay at one or more foreign institutions, for the sake of the cultural experience, or simply to broaden their horizons, in the manner of the classical "grand tour", without consideration of whether going abroad would delay graduation.

There are several reasons for this change in attitudes. One is the advent of mass higher education: whereas many students in the days of elite education may not have had to worry about incurring increased costs by prolonging their studies, most students today need to "get through their studies" as quickly as possible, for financial reasons. Linked to this, there is also a perception that the efficient completion of a study programme with good results is valued by employers. Even if the reasons for prolonging one's studies may be perfectly valid – and broadening one's horizons by spending time abroad should definitely fall into this category – employers seem to be sceptical of prospective employees who divert too strongly from the course chartered by normative study programmes. Not least, today's students see no reason why they would need to choose between completing a study programme on time and taking part of that programme abroad. If studying abroad is an enriching experience, culturally as well as academically, why should this not be acknowledged through the recognition of study periods and qualifications earned aboard?

This shift in attitudes and the increasing political emphasis on the desirability of encouraging academic mobility have led to increasing emphasis on the fair recognition of qualifications. Recognition has moved from being the domain of highly specialised technicians to being a key element of higher education policies. In Europe, recognition is one of the key areas of the Bologna Process, which aims to establish a European Higher Education Area (EHEA) by 2010, and statements on recognition are a regular feature of the communiqués from the ministerial meetings of the Bologna Process. Recognition is also a key area for most higher education institutions, which often employ specialists in the area. In North America, AACRAO[5] – the American Association of Collegiate Registrars and Admissions Officers – sees recognition issues as one of its main concerns, and recognition issues are also high on the agenda of NAFSA: Association of International Educators.[6] In Europe, the

---

5. www.aacrao.org/.
6. www.nafsa.org/.

EAIE – European Association for International Education[7] – has a professional section for admissions officers and credentials evaluators, know as ACE.[8]

The recognition of a foreign qualification is ultimately a legal and/or administrative act, and it is only fitting that the recognition of foreign qualifications should have a legal basis. Worldwide, UNESCO has a set of regional conventions on recognition. For the European Region, the basis is the joint Council of Europe/UNESCO Convention on the Recognition of Qualifications concerning Higher Education in the European Region (known as the Council of Europe/UNESCO Recognition Convention or the Lisbon Recognition Convention; the latter because it was adopted in Lisbon on 11 April 1997).[9] Recognition, as the Lisbon Recognition Convention itself allows, can be established at the institutional, sub-national or national level, depending on the laws and policies of a particular country and education system.

The Lisbon Recogntion Convention is the most recent of the regional recognition conventions, and it sets the current legal standards for the recognition of foreign qualifications. It is in this convention that the concept of substantial differences is found.

The concept of "substantial difference" in the Council of Europe/ UNESCO Recognition Convention

The basic assumption of the convention may be summarised as "foreign qualifications shall be recognised unless the competent recognition authority is able to demonstrate that there is a substantial difference between the qualification for which recognition is sought and the corresponding qualification of the country (or rather, education system) in which recognition is sought".[10]

In other words, if a person seeks recognition of qualification X from country B in country A, the competent recognition authorities of country A may refuse recognition – or grant only partial recognition – if they can demonstrate a substantial difference between qualification X from country B and a similar qualification – qualification Y – from country A.

In the convention, the term "substantial difference" is found in:

Article IV.1

Each Party shall recognize the qualifications issued by other Parties meeting the general requirements for access to higher education in those Parties for the purpose of access to programmes belonging to its higher education system, unless a substantial difference can be shown between the general requirements for access in the Party in which the qualification was obtained and in the Party in which recognition of the qualification is sought.

---

7. www.eaie.org/.
8. www.eaie.org/ACE/ . See also www.aic.lv/ace/.
9. For easy access to all the regional conventions as well as to the subsidiary texts of the Council of Europe/UNESCO Recognition Convention, see www.enic-naric.net/index.aspx?s=n&r=ena&d=legal.
10. This is a paraphrase rather than a quote from the convention.

...

Article IV.3

Where a qualification gives access only to specific types of institutions or programmes of higher education in the Party in which the qualification was obtained, each other Party shall grant holders of such qualifications access to similar specific programmes in institutions belonging to its higher education system, unless a substantial difference can be demonstrated between the requirements for access in the Party in which the qualification was obtained and the Party in which recognition of the qualification is sought.

...

Article V.1

Each Party shall recognize periods of study completed within the framework of a higher education programme in another Party. This recognition shall comprise such periods of study towards the completion of a higher education programme in the Party in which recognition is sought, unless substantial differences can be shown between the periods of study completed in another Party and the part of the higher education programme which they would replace in the Party in which recognition is sought.

...

Article VI.1

To the extent that a recognition decision is based on the knowledge and skills certified by the higher education qualification, each Party shall recognize the higher education qualifications conferred in another Party, unless a substantial difference can be shown between the qualification for which recognition is sought and the corresponding qualification in the Party in which recognition is sought.

The term "substantial difference" clearly indicates that minor differences between qualifications do not provide sufficient reason for non-recognition. It takes account of the diversity of higher education systems and traditions and recognises that there are usually differences between corresponding qualifications in different education systems. Therefore, an assumption of no differences between qualifications would very often make recognition impossible. Thus, the existence of differences between qualifications alone does not provide sufficient reason for non-recognition. This is underlined by the explanatory report to the convention regarding Article IV.1, which says:

> It should be underlined, however, that not any difference with respect to one of these areas should be considered substantial.

The explanatory report further underlines that:

> As a general rule, in assessing whether there is a substantial difference between the two qualifications concerned, Parties and higher education institutions are, however, encouraged to consider, as far as possible, the merits of the individual qualifications in question without having recourse to an automatic comparison of the length of study required to obtain the qualification.

17

And it offers some examples of what might be considered substantial differences in terms of access qualifications:

> A Party may, however, refuse to grant recognition if it can show that there is a substantial difference between its own general requirements for access and those of the Party in which the qualification in question was earned. Such differences may concern the contents of primary and secondary education, some examples of which are:
>
> − a substantial difference between a general education and a specialized technical education;
>
> − a difference in the length of study which substantially affects the curriculum contents;
>
> − the presence, absence or extent of specific subjects, such as prerequisite courses or non-academic subjects;
>
> − a substantial difference in focus, such as between a programme designed primarily for entrance to higher education and a programme designed primarily to prepare for the world of work.

Further guidance in determining what might constitute a substantial difference is offered in the explanatory report to the convention regarding Article VI.1, where it is underlined that such a difference should be both important and relevant to the purpose for which recognition is sought:

> While acknowledging that recognition decisions may entail other factors than the knowledge and skills certified by the higher education qualification, this Article states the basic principle that Parties should recognize higher education qualifications earned in the higher education system of any other Party unless a substantial difference can be shown between the qualification for which recognition is sought and the corresponding qualification in the country in which recognition is sought. It is underlined that the difference must be both substantial and relevant as defined by the competent recognition authority. Recognition cannot be withheld for reasons immaterial to the qualification or the purpose for which recognition is sought. It is the responsibility of the Party or higher education institution wishing to refuse recognition to show that the difference is substantial.

This part of the explanatory report also makes the link between the recognition of qualifications and the formal standing of the institution or programme from which the qualification originates:

> If a considerable part of an applicant's studies for the qualification in question have been undertaken at an institution not recognized as belonging to the higher education system of a Party, the Parties may consider this as constituting a substantial difference in the terms of this Article.

Finally, the explanatory report makes the point regarding Article V.1 that the definition of "substantial difference" is often difficult to establish, and that further work is required in this area:

> This article states the basic principle that periods of study undertaken abroad shall be recognized unless a substantial difference can be shown between the period of study undertaken abroad and the part of the higher education programme which they would

replace. It is the duty of the Party or institution wishing to withhold recognition to show that the differences in question are substantial. This Article makes no distinction between participants in organized mobility programmes and "free movers".

It is realized that it may be more difficult for a competent recognition authority to show the existence of substantial differences in the case of the recognition of periods of study than for the recognition of access qualifications (Section IV) or higher education qualifications (Section VI). There is therefore a need for guidelines on this point; these could be proposed by the ENIC Network, taking into account the experience of higher education institutions. As an example, while account may be taken of quality and major differences in programme content in the definition of "substantial differences", Parties should show sufficient flexibility in their definitions.

The final sentence of this part of the explanatory report is also well worth underlining when considering the concept of "substantial difference":

Attention is specifically drawn to the fact that a narrow definition of the concept of "substantial differences" with regard to course content may easily discourage academic mobility.

As will be clear from the above excerpts, it is up to the competent recognition authority to demonstrate that a substantial difference exists and that it is therefore justified in refusing recognition or in granting partial recognition. It is not up to the applicant to demonstrate that a substantial difference does not exist, and the basic assumption is that the existence of a substantial difference is the exception rather than the rule. An applicant may, however, wish to contest the assertion by a competent recognition authority that a substantial difference does in fact exist, and the convention foresees – in Article III.5 – that applicants have the right to appeal a decision:

Decisions on recognition shall be made within a reasonable time limit specified beforehand by the competent recognition authority and calculated from the time all necessary information in the case has been provided. If recognition is withheld, the reasons for the refusal to grant recognition shall be stated, and information shall be given concerning possible measures the applicant may take in order to obtain recognition at a later stage. If recognition is withheld, or if no decision is taken, the applicant shall be able to make an appeal within a reasonable time limit.

First considerations

On the basis of the text of the convention and the explanatory report, it is possible to establish a number of elements for the further consideration of the concept "substantial difference":

1. The existence of a substantial difference[11] may provide a reason not to recognise a qualification, or to give only partial recognition.

---

11. In this part of the document, the expression "the existence of a substantial difference" and similar expressions should be understood as shorthand for "the existence of a substantial difference between the qualification for which recognition is sought and the corresponding qualification of the country (or rather, education system) in which recognition is sought".

2.   The responsibility for demonstrating the existence of a substantial difference lies with the competent recognition authority assessing the application for recognition.

3.   The existence of a substantial difference provides a reason for non-recognition, but entails no obligation in this sense. A competent recognition authority may choose to recognise a qualification even if it considers that a substantial difference exists. In such cases, it would, however, seem reasonable to assume that other factors may be considered to outweigh the substantial difference and, at first sight, it would also seem reasonable to assume that such cases would be rare.

4.   The difference in question should be substantial in relation to the function of the qualification and the purpose for which recognition is sought.

5.   The real test of whether a difference is "substantial" therefore lies in the function of the qualification and the purpose for which recognition is sought more than in the formal characteristics of the qualification, such as length of study or the architecture of a given study programme.

The elements of a qualification

The emphasis in the convention and its explanatory report on defining "substantial difference" in relation to the function of the qualification and the purpose for which recognition is sought would seem to underline the need to consider the concept of "substantial difference" in the light of how we analyse the concept of "qualification". In a European context at least, considerable work has been undertaken in this respect within the framework of the Bologna Process, in particular through the development of an overarching framework of qualifications for the EHEA.[12] This work was underpinned by two conferences on qualifications structures (Copenhagen, March 2003)[13] and qualifications frameworks (Copenhagen, January 2005).[14] The conference on "Recognition and Credit Systems in the Context of Lifelong Learning" (Prague, June 2003)[15] may also be of relevance.

---

12. For information on qualifications frameworks in the European Higher Education Area, see www. ond.vlaanderen.be/hogeronderwijs/bologna/qf/qf.asp.
13. The general report is available at www.bologna-bergen2005.no/EN/Bol_sem/Old/030327-28Copenhagen/030327-28Report_General_Rapporteur.pdf; the recommendations at www.bologna-bergen2005.no/EN/Bol_sem/Old/030327-28Copenhagen/030327-28CPH_Recommandations.pdf.
14. The general report is available at www.bologna-bergen2005.no/EN/Bol_sem/Seminars/050113-14_General_report.pdf; the recommendations at www.bologna-bergen2005.no/EN/Bol_sem/Seminars/050113-14Copenhagen/050113-14_Recommendations.pdf.
15.The general report is available at www.bologna-bergen2005.no/EN/Bol_sem/Old/030605-07Prague/030605-07General_Report.pdf; the recommendations at www.bologna-bergen2005.no/EN/Bol_sem/Old/030605-07Prague/030605-07Recommendations.pdf.

The report of the first Copenhagen conference and then the report of the working group refer to five elements that combine to make up a qualification:

– level

– workload

– quality

– profile

– learning outcomes.[16]

Level designates the place of a given qualification within an education system or – in keeping with the terminology now adopted within the Bologna Process, but also used in countries like Australia, New Zealand and South Africa – a qualifications framework. Typical examples in national systems are bachelor's, master's and doctoral degrees; the overarching qualifications framework for the EHEA uses the generic terms first, second and third (cycle) degrees.

Workload refers to the amount of work required to successfully complete a unit of learning. The United States and Canada have long expressed workload in terms of credits, and European countries are now also moving away from time (length of study; most often expressed as years of study) to credits, as an expression of workload. Within the Bologna Process, the "currency" for workload is ECTS[17] credits, but some European countries have national credit systems where national credits can be "translated" into ECTS credits. In terms of recognition of North American qualifications in Europe and vice versa, the "translation" between US and Canadian credit systems and the ECTS is an important issue.

Quality indicates that a qualification must not only be of a given level and entail a given workload; it must also be of sufficient quality (it must be "good enough"). The need for a credentials evaluator to know something about the quality of the institution, or the programme from which a qualification originates, provides a strong link between recognition and quality assurance and credentials evaluators need to make use of the outcomes of quality assessment. If an institution or programme has failed a quality assessment, this would provide a reason not to recognise the qualifications issued by the institution or programme. Quality assurance is an increasingly important element of higher education policy, in North America and Europe as well as in other parts of the world, and the outcomes of a quality assurance exercise – whether in the form of formal accreditation, a quality assurance statement or any other form – are important tools for recognition specialists. It should, however, be emphasised that what a credentials evaluator needs to know is whether the institution or programme from which a given qualification emanates is of sufficient quality, that is whether it meets the relevant minimum quality standards. This information can be gleaned from accreditation or similar quality assurance

16. For a detailed exploration, see Sjur Bergan, *Qualifications. Introduction to a Concept,* Council of Europe Higher Education Series No. 6, Council of Europe Publishing, Strasbourg, 2007.
17. European Credit Transfer and Accumulation System.

determinations, or from other analyses that have a legitimate and objective basis. However, the recognition of a qualification should not depend on whether it comes from an institution that is highly ranked in one of the many ranking lists that are now gaining considerable – and in our view, unwarranted – publicity.

Profile can be relevant in two ways. In one sense, profile may refer to the overall orientation of an institution or a study programme, typically in a binary system that distinguishes between universities and non-university institutions. Here, the distinction would generally have to do with the role and prominence of research in the activities of the institution and as an underlying factor in its study programmes, as well as with the extent to which a programme takes a theoretical or applied approach.

The second sense of profile has to do with the individual characteristics of a qualification, for example, a first degree in physics or a second degree in linguistics. With increased flexibility in study programmes and the increased use of credits in most European countries, study programmes in most countries of the European Region now allow for a measure of individual choice that can give graduates an individual profile that goes beyond the choice of a field of specialisation or, in US terms, a major. This has for quite some time been a feature of study programmes in North America. Thus, students may include a number of credits in disciplines that may support their main area of specialisation, or that have nothing to do with their main specialisation. Courses in a foreign language, statistics or law may, depending on the students' specialisation, be examples of both categories of courses.

One important aspect of profile, then, is the balance between specialisation and broader orientation. This is particularly relevant in the context of the recognition of North American qualifications in Europe and vice versa, since many European systems have traditionally emphasised specialisation over broad orientation for first cycle qualifications, whereas the concept of a liberal arts education is an important part of North American – or at least US – higher education at first degree level. Developments in many European systems, with increased possibilities for developing "personal" profiles within the framework of given study programmes, should provide for a greater measure of common ground in this respect.

Learning outcomes describe what a graduate knows and is able to do on the basis of a qualification.[18] Increasingly, the focus of higher education policy debates, as well as the more specific debate on the recognition of qualifications, emphasises learning outcomes over the formal structures of study programmes.[19] This is a challenge to recognition specialists, because learning outcomes are often more difficult

---

18. For an excellent introduction, see Stephen Adam, "An Introduction to Learning Outcomes: A Consideration of the Nature, Function and Position of Learning Outcomes in the Creation of the European Higher Education Area", article B.2-3.1, in Eric Froment, Jürgen Kohler, Lewis Purser and Lesley Wilson (eds), *EUA Bologna Handbook – Making Bologna Work*, Raabe Verlag, Berlin, 2006.
19. Learning outcomes are explicitly referred to in the Recommendation on Criteria and Procedures for the Assessment of Foreign Qualifications and Periods of Study, paragraph 37, and in the corresponding part of the explanatory memorandum to this recommendation.

to describe and assess. While length of study is perhaps not the most meaningful criterion, it is a relatively straightforward one.

Qualifications frameworks

Qualifications frameworks describe how individual qualifications in a given education system fit together and how learners can move between qualifications. Such movement is most often thought of in terms of "upward mobility" – students progress from a first degree to a second degree – but it can also be sideways, or even from a higher to a lower cycle in cases where learners change their speciality or orientation.

While all education systems have qualifications frameworks, "new style" qualifications frameworks, as perceived within the EHEA, are explicit in describing qualifications in terms of learning outcomes (although other elements may also be included in the description) and the articulation between the different qualifications that make up the framework.

Within the EHEA, ministers in Bergen adopted an overarching framework of qualifications, which consists of three levels. Countries may include intermediate qualifications in their national frameworks. The overarching framework, as adopted in Bergen, is reproduced on page 131.[20]

The concept of a qualifications framework is relevant to the consideration of substantial differences because it provides a framework for the comparison of qualifications across the borders of an education system. If a given education system describes a given qualification as a first cycle degree (for example, country Z describes qualification A as a first cycle degree in its own qualifications framework), that gives a strong indication that other countries should recognise this qualification as a first cycle degree. If they do not want to give such recognition, they would need to justify their position by demonstrating a substantial difference between this qualification and their own first cycle qualification(s).

While the EHEA's overarching framework of qualifications does not apply to all countries of the European Region, it may nevertheless provide a useful framework against which to consider the concept of "substantial difference". It is also worth noting that while many countries, including the United States and Canada, do not have a qualifications framework and do not plan to develop one, they nevertheless provide descriptions of their degree system that have many elements in common with qualifications frameworks.

The articulation between qualifications is also important, because this may be an element in the assessment of a foreign qualification. The clearest example concerns recognition of qualifications that give access to a regulated profession, where

---

20. The full report of the working group may be found at www.bologna-bergen2005.no/Docs/00-Main_doc/050218_QF_EHEA.pdf.

requirements are very clearly linked to the successful completion of given study programmes and the obtaining of given degrees (possibly supplemented by the completion of a practice period after obtaining the necessary degree). However, within a qualifications framework, the description of a given qualification could include a description of the qualifications and/or learning outcomes normally required for access to study programmes leading to the qualification, as well as the access to further qualifications a given qualification would normally give. In some cases, a description of the type of access a given qualification gives to the labour market may also be provided, whereas in some countries institutions or recognition authorities are prevented by law or regulations from providing such information.

Within qualifications frameworks, several different "learning paths" may lead to the same qualification. While reference is sometimes made to "lifelong learning qualifications", these should – at least at higher education level – more properly be seen as different learning paths leading to one of the qualifications contained in a national qualifications framework.

While the convention does not refer to qualifications frameworks, it is clear that they constitute a significant development in the way many parties to the convention see their qualifications and degree systems, and all parties to the convention that are also members of the Bologna Process have launched work on their national qualifications frameworks. Bologna members have also committed to completing their national frameworks and even if one might reasonably suspect that a number of countries may require some more time, qualifications frameworks will be an important feature of the European Region within the next few years. However, as stated above, some countries – those that are not members of the Bologna Process – may choose not to develop formal qualifications frameworks and, for years to come, credentials evaluators will also be faced with qualifications that date from before the introduction of qualifications frameworks. Qualifications frameworks, as a way of defining the functions of qualifications and their relationship within a given system, will therefore be an important feature of the context in which the convention will be applied.

Attitudes to recognition

The issue of substantial differences is also important because attitudes to recognition seem to vary considerably throughout the European Region. In another context, this has been referred to as "two cultures",[21] one of which emphasises the identification of pragmatic solutions within a given legal framework and seeks to apply a measure of "common sense", while the other emphasises the authority of legal provisions and seeks to apply a relatively rigid interpretation of these provisions.[22]

---

21. Sjur Bergan, "A Tale of Two Cultures in Higher Education Policies: the Rule of Law or an Excess of Legalism?", *Journal of Studies in International Education*, Volume 8, Issue 2 (Summer 2004).
22. See also Sjur Bergan and Sandra Ferreira, "Implementation of the Lisbon Recognition Convention and Contributions to the Bologna Process", in Sjur Bergan (ed.), *Recognition Issues in the Bologna Process*, Council of Europe Publishing, Strasbourg, 2003.

The difference in attitudes can also be looked at from a different angle: one can be characterised as emphasising the needs and interests of individual applicants, which would entail a propensity to recognise applicants' qualifications to the fullest extent possible, whereas the other can be characterised as emphasising the need to uphold and protect the education system and standards of the home country, which would entail a propensity not to recognise foreign qualifications, unless the credentials evaluator is absolutely convinced they are equal to the corresponding qualifications of the home country.

It should be underlined that while there may be differences in national and cultural traditions with regard to the interpretation of legal provision – some cultures may be seen as more rule-bound than others – this is not solely a question of national and cultural background. There will also be considerable variation between individuals within the same country or administrative culture.

It follows from this that credentials evaluators will most likely be inclined to interpret the concept of substantial differences according to national and cultural traditions, the cultures of the bureaucracies and organisations in which they work, the policy frameworks – restrictive or flexible – under which they work, and the knowledge, experience and personal biases which they possess. Whereas some will seek to interpret the concept broadly, others will seek to give a narrow interpretation. Some will prefer to err on the side of generosity towards the individual applicant, whereas others will prefer to err on the side of caution.

Some of the differences in attitudes and practice may stem from the double function of recognition. On the one hand, recognition of foreign qualifications is an instrument to ensure fair access policies and to make sure that applicants are admitted to study programmes and occupations in which they have a fair chance to succeed. There is also a strong aspect of public protection in the case of regulated professions, in particular, since the regulated professions tend to be occupations in which malpractice can have grave and immediate consequences. On the other hand, recognition is a tool for promoting academic mobility and mobility in the labour market.

The recognition of qualifications may also be considered as a public service, since regardless of the organisational model and status of individual competent recognition authorities, it is carried out with a public mandate. As such, it is subject to the increasing demands on public service that seem to be a general feature of most of our societies, and which tend to emphasise individual rights and aspirations.

Differences in attitudes to recognition persist, and they are an important issue. In general terms, one major goal of the work of the ENIC and NARIC networks is to promote flexible attitudes and to move away from rigid and "legalistic" interpretations of legal provisions. More broadly, one would hope that credentials evaluators at higher education institutions see their tasks in the same light.

Some questions for consideration

If the five elements of qualifications outlined above, as well as the concept of qualifications frameworks, are considered useful, they may help guide credentials evaluators and policy makers in their consideration of substantial differences.

The first question to be asked when considering substantial differences would be where in a qualifications framework should a given qualification be placed? Is qualification A a first degree, a second degree or a third degree, or is it a qualification giving access to higher education? If it is an intermediate qualification, where should it be situated? Is it an intermediate qualification within the first cycle, within the second cycle or within the third cycle?

If the competent authorities of the education system, within which a qualification has been issued, have indicated its place within the qualifications framework of that system, this should reasonably be the point of departure for the assessment of the given foreign qualification. If no such indication has been provided, the competent recognition authority of the country in which recognition is sought would most likely seek to establish the place of the qualification within its own qualifications framework, where this exists, or within its own degree system.

Once the recognition authority has broadly determined the place of a given qualification within a qualifications framework (or within its degree system where no "new style" qualifications framework exists), it may assess whether the foreign qualification is substantially different from its own qualification(s) that fall within the same category in its own qualifications framework.

In so doing, it is suggested the authority should refer to the elements that make up a qualification. This part of the document is intended to outline some issues credentials evaluators and policy makers may wish to consider in this respect. They were also the basis for the project that led to this book, and which engaged the ENIC and NARIC networks in very substantive discussions over three annual meetings. The questions are nevertheless not intended to be exhaustive and readers may well wish to add questions and elements of their own for consideration. The questions are intended to launch a debate, not to limit it.

Level

If a given qualification is designated by the competent authorities of the country of origin as being of a given level (for example, second cycle), what might constitute a substantial difference justifying non-recognition or partial recognition?

How close is the relationship between level and workload?

How should intermediate qualifications be assessed, particularly in systems that do not have corresponding intermediary qualifications?

Workload

Can substantial differences in level be determined with reference to workload alone? If yes, what constitutes a substantial difference?[23]

Do all components of a given qualification need to be of the same level? If not, how much can be of a different (lower) level? (Cf. the overarching qualifications framework of the EHEA, which stipulates that second cycle degrees "[t]ypically include 90-120 ECTS credits, with a minimum of 60 credits at the level of the second cycle".)

Quality

If an education provider has not been quality-assessed, or if the results of a quality assessment have not been made publicly available, should this be considered a substantial difference?

How can the provider in this case possibly compensate for the lack of an independent quality assessment?

In view of the increased emphasis on quality assurance in the higher education policy debate since the convention was adopted in 1997, is it now conceivable that a party might be able to fulfil its obligation under Section VIII, concerning provision of information on the institutions and programmes that make up its higher education system, without making reference to the outcomes of external quality assurance?

Profile

To what extent and for what purposes can a difference in field of study (for example, mathematics and physics, or political science and Japanese), or in the composition of a qualification within the same broad field of study (for example, between a business graduate with additional competence in a given foreign language and one with additional competence in statistics) be considered a substantial difference?

To what extent, and for what purposes, can a difference in the general orientation of the institution or programme (for example, between university and non-university higher education) be considered a substantial difference?

To what extent, and for what purposes, can a difference between a high degree of specialisation versus a broad orientation be considered a substantial difference?

Learning outcomes

How can the assessment of substantial differences be focused, as far as possible, on potential differences in learning outcomes?

---

23. In terms of access qualifications, on Article IV.1 the explanatory report refers to "a difference in the length of study which substantially affects the curriculum content".

To what extent can similarities in learning outcomes overcome possible differences in level or workload?

How can learning outcomes be assessed in systems that have not (yet) provided descriptions of learning outcomes for their qualifications? Conversely, how can such systems assess foreign qualifications on the basis of learning outcomes where a description of these is provided for the foreign qualification for which recognition is sought?

Formal rights

Can a difference in the formal rights granted to holders of a given qualification be considered a substantial difference?[24]

If the learning outcomes, level, workload, quality and profile of a foreign degree are roughly similar to that of the corresponding qualification of the country in which recognition is sought, but the latter grants the holder formal rights (for example with regards to exercising a given profession or line of work) whereas the foreign qualification does not, may this be considered a substantial difference? If it can, how can the holder of the foreign qualification address the difference?

Conversely, if a qualification does not give the holder certain rights in the home country, but such rights are granted to holders of similar qualifications in the country in which recognition is sought, should the lack of formal rights in the home country be construed as a substantial difference? An example might be that, in certain countries, holders of certain first degrees, such as those from (some or all) non-university higher education programmes, do not have access to second degree study programmes. If holders of such a qualification apply for recognition in a country where holders of similar qualifications have access to second degree programmes, should the difference in formal rights be an argument for non-recognition or partial recognition? In the latter case, what measures could the applicant take to earn full recognition? In practice, many countries seem not to consider the lack of formal rights as a substantial difference in such cases.

Attitudes to recognition

How can a common understanding of the concept of "substantial difference" be developed in view of differences in attitudes to recognition?

* * *

These questions were the starting point for the project that led to this book, and the pages that follow will point to many factors for an answer. Nevertheless, there is

---

24. The Recommendation on Criteria and Procedures for the Assessment of Foreign Qualifications and Periods of Study states in paragraph 38 that: "Where formal rights attach to a certain foreign qualification in the home country, the qualification should be evaluated with a view to giving the holder comparable formal rights in the host country, in so far as these exist and they arise from the knowledge and skills certified by the qualification".

no definitive or "right" answer. While many interpretations of what might constitute a substantial difference are clearly wrong and emphasise minor rather than substantial differences, there are areas where well-qualified credentials evaluators may reasonably disagree. This book aims to outline some possibilities and above all to stimulate thinking and discussion around the crucial concept of substantial differences. No legal text can provide an exhaustive definition of the concept and not even a book-length discussion can give an exhaustive illustration.

II. Examples and cases

Basil College of Catering: study duration and differences in programme profile as "substantial differences"?

Peter J. Wells and Rolf Lofstad

Introduction

One of the more frequently cited rationales for concluding a "substantial difference" between qualifications or awarding institutions is the duration of study programmes. Within the countries of the ENIC and NARIC networks (Europe, North America, Israel, New Zealand and Australia), the minimum duration of full-time study to complete a first, second and even third cycle degree can vary widely. Typically, for example, a bachelor's degree in the United States requires at least four years full-time enrolment, while in the United Kingdom the norm has traditionally been three years, and in parts of continental Europe, particularly in the systems of central and eastern European countries, a first cycle degree has taken up to five years to complete. At the same time, almost all national systems include a number of programme profiles which require additional study periods at partner institutions, or a language component undertaken in another country, or a mandatory work-placement/internship period, or a combination of all three – any of which can substantially prolong the minimum time to completion of the qualification.

Adding to the confusion of comparisons are the harmonising effects of the Bologna Process in Europe, which are increasingly giving rise to credentials evaluators being faced with comparing so-called shorter "new Bologna" degrees with longer "pre-Bologna" degrees, programmes and structures. With so many variables and individual characteristics of seemingly similar programmes, assessing the possibilities for recognition often requires a more thorough investigation than simple comparisons of length of study.

The case study approach and methodology

In order to investigate how different credentials evaluators approach the issues of study duration when assessing qualifications from one country compared to another, or of one institution with another, in the same national contexts, a case study (see Fig. 1) was designed for discussion. The case was based on a real example, but with fictional institutes, qualifications and non-defined countries. The overarching question to be addressed was whether or not a qualification which traditionally takes a longer period of full-time study to complete in one institution constitutes a substantial difference to that in another which takes a longer or shorter time. In addition, the two fictitious qualifications presented in this case were elaborated to show clear differences in the profile and content of the programmes, for example, with regard to the inclusion, or not, of a professional practice period.

The case was presented and debated during study workshops at the 14th Joint Annual Meeting of the ENIC and NARIC networks in Bucharest in 2007. Two independent groups of credentials evaluators from 20 different countries in the European Region were asked to consider the case and two related questions. From the outset, it was emphasised that there were to be no right or wrong answers to the case or the prompt questions, and that the purpose of the discussion was to express personal opinions, describe actual practices and benefit from a mutual learning dialogue of good practice.

Fig. 1. Comparing qualifications – a case study

Institution	Basil College of Catering (BCC)	Fawlty Institute of Travel and Tourism (FITT)
Country	X	Y
V1	First level degree pro-gramme: "BA in Hospitality Management"	First level degree programme: "Diploma in Hotel and Hospitality Management"
V2	Programme duration – four years	Programme duration – three years
V3	Students must take a six-month work placement during their studies	There is no work placement requirement
V4	Students must take at least two semesters at a partner institution in one of three different countries	Students take all their courses at FITT
V5	Students study full time on a semester basis	Students study full time on a trimester basis
V6	BCC is fully recognised and the programme accredited in the three other countries where it has joint study arrangements	FITT is fully recognised and accredited in Country Y
V7	Students have 20 hours contact time per week, for 35 weeks per year	Students have 24 hours contact time per week, for 40 weeks per year
V8	Students must accumulate 180 credit hours in order to graduate from the programme	Students must accumulate 180 credit hours in order to graduate from the programme
V9	BCC has a library with 100 000 volumes	FITT has a library with 50 000 volumes

Institution	Basil College of Catering (BCC)	Fawlty Institute of Travel and Tourism (FITT)
Country	X	Y
V10	BCC has state-of-the-art ICT facilities	FITT has state-of-the-art ICT facilities
Q1	If you were asked to assess the equivalency of qualifications received from BCC and FITT, what additional information would you need to know, in order to undertake an accurate assessment?	
Q2	Based on the above and any further information you might receive, which factors would you consider to be (a) substantial differences, and (b) not substantial differences?	

Note: V= variable; Q= question.
Source: the authors.

Results of the case study analysis

The following provides a synthesis of the discussions and recommendations from both groups, on the issues outlined in the two qualifications and their responses to the two questions posed by the authors.

Institutional facilities

Factors such as the size of the institution, enrolment numbers, history, longevity, library collections, ICT facilities and other institutional characteristics were considered unanimously to be irrelevant in assessing equivalencies.

Country of the issuing institution

There was general agreement that the home country of each institution was also unimportant. However, some participants acknowledged that this could be an "influencing" factor. Some members stated that they could not fail to approach the decision process with a more positive predisposition, when they were confronted with a qualification from a country they "knew to have a good higher education system". When debating this point, it was nevertheless agreed that this human factor, however involuntary, did not follow the spirit of the Lisbon convention and that every credential, regardless of its issuing country, should always be approached objectively and without any notions of preconceived assumptions.

Work placement/internship requirements

The work placement element included in the programme at the Basil College of Catering (BCC) was considered by some to be a definite substantial difference, yet for others, it was irrelevant. It was clear that for those who believed it to be a "substantial difference", it was substantial in the pejorative sense, rather than a positive difference. Those who saw it as irrelevant viewed the work placement as simply a reflection of a different course structure to that offered by the Fawlty Institute of Travel and Tourism (FITT), and it therefore had no bearing on the question of recognition. Interestingly, the participants who saw this element as irrelevant also admitted that, it depending on the purpose of the applicant's request for recognition (for example, work or further study), a work placement element may actually benefit the applicant's chances of finding employment or accessing a further course of study, but that this was, nevertheless, not a matter for them to judge in their capacity of establishing equivalency of the credential.

Study periods at a partner institution

This element provoked a very similar discussion to the debate on internships. The period of study at a partner institution described in the qualification from BCC was seen by some respondents as a substantial difference. As with the internship question, there seemed to be confusion between the terms "difference" and "substantial difference", as it is referred to in the convention. It is clear that the two programmes are "different" and that it would be extremely unlikely for them to be identical. But establishing that factors like these constitute a "substantial difference" in the credential holders' ability to undertake further study, or employment in the field, is doubtful. Further information on the types of "partner institutions" of BCC, in terms of their accreditation and recognition status, might be useful according to some discussants. For the majority, however, the only proviso was that BCC itself be recognised in its own country and/or that the programme it offers is fully accredited. If this was indeed the case, it was felt that a lengthy investigation of the partnering institutions was unnecessary for establishing equivalency.

Programme contact time

Considering the issue of contact time, one participant calculated that the contact time at BCC totalled 600 hours compared to 940 at FITT. Again, this could be seen as a significant difference, this time in favour of the programme offered by FITT. Other participants challenged this notion. Is this really significant? Is contact time the same as credits, as described in the ECTS or similar systems? If the question of recognition rests purely on contact time, then the answer would be yes. However, both groups concluded that such details are irrelevant to the quality of graduates, their eventual learning outcomes, or the overall rigour of a given programme. Quite clearly, the BCC programme operates on a semester basis versus the trimester system of FITT, and the internship and study abroad requirements at BCC must, by design, reduce the contact time students have with their home institution. On the face of it, this element might seem essential to an accurate evaluation, but on closer inspection, it too is unimportant to evaluators. Secondly, guessing whether or not this element is of importance to a receiving institution or employer is not the role of an evaluator in this case.

Learning outcomes

Neither of the qualifications presented in the case provided any concrete learning or graduate outcomes. Information about the learning and/or graduate learning outcomes, preferably in the form of a Diploma Supplement style format, was considered by everybody to be the crucial missing information needed to make a fair and accurate judgment on the case.

Other "missing information"

Suggestions were also made for supplementary information on such areas as: the language of instruction in each programme; the inclusion of a thesis element; whether or not the programmes were accredited to external professional associations; the position of each institution in their respective national qualifications framework; and the system of institutional/programme accreditation in each country. It was, however, agreed that none of these were necessarily essential, nor would they alone constitute a deciding factor in the search for establishing equivalency.

Programme duration

Having investigated the facts presented in the case, both groups were then asked to state whether or not they believed that the differing programme durations (four years at BCC versus three years at FITT) were grounds for not granting equivalency on the basis of "substantial difference". The unanimous opinion was that the length of study, though an initial indicator, did not reflect the full picture of either qualification, and thus taking such information in isolation could undermine the meaning of the Lisbon Recognition Convention and result in an erroneous decision. However, according to some participants, personal opinions are sometimes irrelevant in the practice of their respective centres or offices. Many commented that since programme duration for first cycle degrees in their countries is strictly legislated, they would not be in a position to grant equivalency to the qualification from the FITT which did not meet this criterion, regardless of any other factors such as programme profile. Accordingly, the same situation often also arises with second and third cycle qualifications. Some participants felt powerless to address these contradictions between national legislation and their country signing and/or ratifying the Lisbon Recognition Convention.

Conclusions

On the surface, the two qualifications in this case appear comparable, yet not entirely the same. The titles of both suggest a similar programme, but the duration differences require more careful examination in order to fully understand how they are constructed. Presentation of detailed learning outcomes would offer an evaluator immeasurable help in reaching a fair and accurate assessment. The issuing country of the qualification is irrelevant, as are incidental factors such as institutional size, longevity or facilities.

Yet, certain questions remain as to whether such a judgment would always be made in cases like these: does national legislation permit an evaluator to follow their professional mandate, based on the facts and factors they are presented with? Is it indeed the role of an evaluator to decide on whether or not an applicant has the necessary capacity for further study on a related or unrelated course, and/or the skills to perform effectively in the field of their qualifications? Does it, in practice, make a difference where the qualification was issued?

Unfortunately, it would seem that the interpretation of "substantial differences", is still all too often highly subjective. While such practices remain, they represent a barrier to the full and impartial implementation of the spirit of the Lisbon Recognition Convention.

References

14th Joint Meeting of ENIC/NARIC networks, and 4th Meeting of the Intergovernmental Committee of the Lisbon Recognition Convention, Bucharest, Romania, 17-19 June 2007.

"The European Higher Education Area" (Bologna Declaration), Joint Declaration of the Ministers of Education, Bologna, 19 June 1999.

Council of Europe and UNESCO, "Convention on the Recognition of Qualifications concerning Higher Education in the European Region", Lisbon, 1997.

European Commission, Council of Europe and UNESCO-CEPES, "The Diploma Supplement",1999.

Different qualification routes to practise a licensed profession: the story of mugwumps

E. Stephen Hunt

Professional qualifications present several unique challenges to competent recognition authorities and credentials evaluators. These can be summarised as follows:

–   Recognition must take into account not only the educational aspects of the qualification, but also the requirements for licensure to practise the profession for which the qualification is intended as preparation, but which may include additional expectations besides the qualification itself.

–   Legal requirements for licensure are often expressed in terms of strict domestic stipulations, and thus limit the discretion of recognition authorities with respect to deviations from the letter of the regulations.

–   Countries sometimes have radically different routes to licensure, especially for technical and commercial services professions but sometimes others as well, and these differences can present challenges in determining the comparability of different qualifications.

–   The final decision concerning the acceptability of a professional qualification, presented for licensure purposes, may fall outside the jurisdiction of the competent recognition authority for educational qualifications, possibly resulting in different judgments by different authorities.

Three different types of qualification routes are examined in this case study. All, in their respective national contexts, lead to qualifications that are accepted by domestic authorities as preparation for licensure in the same profession. The work expected of entry-level professionals in this fictitious field, "mugwumpery", is essentially the same in all three countries. In fact, practising professionals in this field can and have worked side by side on several occasions. At the same time, however, the routes taken in each country to prepare for the profession are quite different.

In one case, the requisite qualification is offered by providers deemed to be higher education institutions and takes the form of a university level first degree. In another, the requisite qualification is earned in a post-secondary institution that is not considered university level and that is legally considered to be vocational education. And in a third, the requisite qualification may be earned outside the formal academic environment, by completing training and practical work experience and sitting progressively more advanced examinations (including supervised work) overseen by professional associations, with the final qualification stage being legally considered to be equivalent to a first degree for employment purposes.

Case study description

A credentials evaluator in country X is presented with two qualifications pertaining to the same regulated profession from country Y and country Z.

The qualification from country Y is awarded by the National Training Scheme for Registered Mugwumps (NTSRM). This is not an academic institution, but rather a professional society recognised in country Y as providing training and examinations that fulfil the requirements to practice mugwumpery. NTRSM qualifications are regarded as equivalent to a degree in the same or a related field. The individual presenting this qualification has 20 years of experience as a senior technician and has been recruited by a leading firm in country X.

The qualification from country Z is regarded as a secondary vocational award in that country, although its content resembles the tertiary programme for mugwumpery in country X, as well as in neighbouring countries. The laws of country Z restrict tertiary professional qualifications to a few designated programmes offered by designated universities, with all other educational programmes being legally regarded as pre-university. The individual presenting this qualification is an experienced mugwump, who has worked alongside colleagues from country X in international settings and seeks permission to work in country X.

In country X, a mugwumpery qualification is earned from a higher education institution and is a degree award in a professional field. The mugwumpery first degree, with specified credits earned, is a requirement to work as a mugwump in country X.

The known facts can be summarised in the following table:

Item description	Country X	Country Y	Country Z
Qualification	Bachelor of Science in Mugwumpery	Diploma in Mugwumpery	Title of Registered Mugwump
Issuing institution	Accredited and recognised tertiary institution (following regular admission to higher education)	Higher vocational school (following one of several possible school-leaving certificates)	National training scheme (a professional body authorised to prepare candidates following school; access requirements flexible)

Item description	Country X	Country Y	Country Z
ECTS credits	120 (normal first cycle degree); with 80 specified credits in defined prerequisite areas	Uncertain. The national policy permits transfer of 60 credits to a degree programme, but the stipulated time of study for the diploma is as long as a first cycle degree and includes all of the 80 specified subject credits defined by country X	Uncertain. The training programme is not expressed in credits, but conversion to credits is possible and country Z permits entry to further degree studies for qualified mugwumps with at least three years of experience and "high pass" on the final examinations
Diploma Supplement	Yes	Vocational DS	Information may be requested from ENIC/NARIC
Additional information	Accreditation is both institutional and programmatic	Accreditation is programmatic	Accreditation of providers and certification of graduates is via the inspectorate for the profession
Additional applicant information	Licensure is awarded following the degree, professional examinations and two years of supervised work experience	The applicant is licensed, has five years' experience and has a job offer from the country X firm in whose office she has been working in her country	The applicant is a licensed senior fellow of the Mugwump Society and has managed a firm in his country that employs country X mugwumps for over 10 years

Discussion questions

Case study participants were asked to consider five questions:

1. If you were the country X evaluator, what additional information would you need in order to fairly assess each of these cases?

2. Assuming that the additional information is obtained, what factors in each case would you consider to be: (a) substantial differences that prevent recognition and (b) differences that do not hinder recognition and for which allowances can be made?

3. If alternative paths exist to a qualification, such as non-academic training and examinations versus academic study, how should the non-academic programme be assessed? Can outcomes trump recognition requirements, demanding degrees or credits?

4. If substantially the same qualification is offered in two countries, but at different levels in each system, how should this be addressed? Can outcomes trump level distinctions?

5. Are national legislation or policy regarding the qualification to work in a given occupation always a barrier to recognition? What would you recommend?

Discussion and conclusions

The case was one of the first to be presented by the Working Party on Substantial Differences, and both the turnout for the case session and the intensity of discussion were somewhat disappointing. Those who did participate tended to divide into two groups: (1) evaluators who felt constrained by regulatory restrictions; and (2) those who came from environments where a degree of discretion was traditional and who saw their role as evaluating the comparability of the qualifications, rather than determining the licensure outcome.

For about half of the discussants, the recognition issues hinged on comparing national laws and the definition of level. They focused on how each country defined the institutions providing the education and training and how this compared to the requirements in country X. On this basis, they tended towards denial of full recognition for both country Y and country Z applicants. In the case of country Y, this was because that system did not define the education as higher education. Content, purpose and outcome were not as important as the description of the providers as "vocational" and "non-university." And, in the case of country Z, the insoluble problem was that the programme lay outside the education system per se. Interestingly, the fact that country Z deemed the programme to be legally equivalent to a degree level course did not trump the fact that it was a non-credit, non-academic process – meaning that in this case it was country X's laws that were considered to trump those of country Z for licensure purposes. The discussants who held these views did remark that their view might change if either country Y or Z had a mutual recognition agreement for mugwumpery with country X.

The other discussants tended to ask questions rather than state conclusions. They were also interested in the possibility of mutual recognition agreements (not in the fact pattern), but they wanted to know more about how authorities in countries Y and Z assigned credit and whether mugwump graduates had access to further study at university level. They also focused on outcomes issues – including the fact that the purpose of the qualifications and the post-licence practice levels were similar. These participants tended towards granting at least partial recognition in the case of country Y, in view of the fact that holders of the diploma could transfer to university programmes. The case of country Z was considered more problematic, because of the difficulty of recognising experiential learning as constituting a degree, particularly in the absence of assigned credits. In both cases, these discussants felt that they could advise country Y and country Z graduates on ways to make up deficiencies that might satisfy licensure requirements. The second group of discussants also felt that the decision of the licensing authorities would trump their evaluations, so that if mutual working arrangements existed, the persons could probably practise at some level, notwithstanding their educational differences.

In summary, the discussion of the mugwump case revealed a similar divide on recognition issues to that discussed in other case studies, as well as those reflected in the NARIC survey described by Bas Wegewijs. There is a "legalistic" camp and a "flexible" camp. The legalistic camp tends to narrowly follow national practice and searches for precise equivalence, granting recognition only if such equivalence can be proven, notwithstanding the more modern concept of recognition as an active rather than a passive decision. It is interesting, however, that the legalistic approach will sometimes ignore educational comparability, so long as a competent professional body accepts a licence in one country as sufficient grounds for permitting practice in another, notwithstanding any educational differences. Flexible authorities, on the other hand, do not look first to whether there is a hard rule to follow or whether a foreign qualification is precisely equivalent in some or all respects to a domestic qualification. Rather, they accept that no two systems produce similar qualifications and their procedural terms of reference give them the discretion to look at the purpose and outcomes of a qualification. They may even ignore level issues if it is obvious that the purpose, content and outcome (licensure) of a professional qualification produce a practitioner who is doing the same job as a national citizen, notwithstanding how his or her national system treats the educational programme.

Substantial differences: Diploma in Medical Radiation Technology

Yves E. Beaudin

Introduction

In 2006, during a regular meeting of the ENIC Bureau and the NARIC Advisory Board (NAB), discussions were held on how to explain to the networks the notion of substantial differences, referred to in the Council of Europe/UNESCO Convention on the Recognition of Qualifications concerning Higher Education in the European Region (Lisbon Recognition Convention).[25] This discussion was initiated thanks to the Italian ENIC/NARIC, which had pointed out, during a meeting of the NARIC Network in November 2005, that the interpretation of this concept varied considerably and that it would be advantageous if a discussion was initiated to clarify this concept. At this meeting, the ENIC Bureau and the NAB decided that a convention recommendation or code explaining substantial differences was not necessarily the favoured approach to explain the concept and that an exchange of practices might best serve the two networks. A Working Party on Substantial Differences was thus created to facilitate discussions within the two networks on this important concept.

Following the ENIC Bureau/NAB meeting, we received a request from a distraught North American medical radiation technologist, whose credentials had been rejected by the competent assessment authorities of a European country. This individual had been offered a position in a European hospital, but this person's qualifications and competencies could not be recognised, due to existing legislation. After analysing the situation, it appeared that this individual's situation clearly demonstrated the complexity surrounding the application of substantial differences during assessment processes.

The medical radiation technologist had been offered a job as chief radiation technologist and primary specialist in a European hospital. The position was a perfect fit, given the candidate's training and expertise as chief of a radiation technology laboratory, professor in a post-secondary higher education institution and many years of experience as a technologist. This individual was also familiar with the new equipment that had been purchased by the hospital and had been offered the position after undergoing a long process to validate her competencies. When the hospital requested governmental authorisation to proceed, it was informed that the credentials of the chosen medical radiation technologist had to be assessed by a central assessment agency.

---

25. Council of Europe/UNESCO Convention on the Recognition of Qualifications concerning Higher Education in the European Region at http://www.cicic.ca/docs/Lisboa/lisbon1997.en.pdf.

During the annual joint meeting of the ENIC/NARIC networks, held in Tallinn on 5 and 6 June 2006, the participants were invited by the Working Party on Substantial Differences to discuss the concept of "Substantial Differences: Toward a Common Understanding?" The case study of the medical radiation technologist that was proposed for discussion follows.

Case study – medical radiation technologist

Case description

A credentials evaluator in country X is presented with a medical radiation technology diploma from a recognised and quality-assured non-degree granting higher education institution from country Y.

Country X does not recognise the credentials of the individual because the diploma was not awarded by a recognised university degree granting institution in country Y. The medical radiation technologist is thus refused access to the profession in country X.

The medical radiation technology programme in country Y is quality assured and recognised by the medical community. Country X offers a similar programme. It also is quality-assured and recognised. It is offered in a university degree granting institution.

Medical authorities in country X want to hire the medical radiation technologist from country Y. During the selection process they analysed the courses taken and recognised the competencies of the medical radiation technologist of country Y. They were also impressed by the labour market experience of the candidate. Nevertheless, the credential had to be formally evaluated by country X.

Discussion questions

1. If you were the credentials evaluator in country X, how would you proceed to validate the credentials and the competencies of the medical radiation technologist from country Y?

2. If the profession is regulated in one country and non-regulated in another, would this have an impact on the credential recognition process?

3. What factors would you consider to be (a) substantial differences and (b) not substantial differences? Does the fact that the programme in country X is given in a university degree granting institution and the programme in country Y in a non-degree granting higher education institution mean that there are substantial differences?

4. What should be required of the medical radiation technologist from country Y to obtain professional recognition in country X, and why?

5.   If competent medical authorities have looked at the learning outcomes and have concluded that there are no substantial differences, what would you do or what can you do in your country as a credentials evaluator?

Discussion

The case study was an excellent stimulus and a revelation to many members of the ENIC and NARIC networks during the discussions in Tallinn. It raised many questions regarding the concept of substantial differences. Participants noted that traditional reference points were changing rapidly and that perhaps this concept had to be taken into account when assessing a foreign qualification.

The case clearly demonstrated that it is not always easy to obtain recognition of qualifications when employers must submit their professional choices to a legal body that cannot always assess competencies because of the technicalities of the law. The country in question had to abide by formal articles of the law, based on levels of study, which hindered recognition. The law made it impossible for an assessor to take into account an individual's expertise, even if the potential employer had deemed the competencies equivalent to the job requirements and the classification scales within their sector. Could the application of the concept of substantial differences have resolved this unfortunate situation?

The study is a good example of some of the issues faced by credential assessors during the evaluation of a credential. Faced with the reality of two very different educational systems,[26] one from Europe and one from North America, the validation of the credentials of the medical radiation technologist appears at first to be difficult to resolve. The difficulties arose from the fact that the intricacies of formal legalistic texts limited assessment to the interpretation of levels and not to competencies. Was this the best approach to favour? The assessment of the medical radiation technologist was not necessarily fair and appeared practically impossible to assess, given that the country doing the assessment required that the individual's qualification should have been taken in a degree granting post-secondary higher education institution.

Such a requirement is not realistic when we know that in North American countries the same programme is usually offered in quality assured non-degree granting post-secondary higher education institutions. If countries in North America and Europe understood uniformly the concept of substantial differences, as defined in the Lisbon Recognition Convention, they would readily recognise that there are no substantial differences to consider when assessing the credentials of a medical radiation technologist trained in a North American non-degree granting post-secondary higher

---

26. "Educational systems" is used here to describe what many countries now call "qualifications frameworks". During the period in which these discussions were held, few countries in Europe and North America had well-articulated qualifications frameworks. We believe that once the frameworks are widely implemented, they may facilitate the application of substantial differences in the assessment of credentials.

education institution, which advantageously compares to qualifications earned in a European degree granting higher education institution. One can easily establish that substantial differences are negligible and equivalent competencies are easily demonstrable. Often, the number of years of study is equivalent, even though this should not be the only criterion when assessing competencies.

Article IV.1 of the Lisbon Recognition Convention is quite clear in its explanation of the notion of substantial differences. In its explanatory report, competent authorities are invited "to consider as far as possible, the merits of the individual qualifications in question without having recourse to an automatic comparison of the length of study required to obtain the qualification ... [and] in assessing whether there is a substantial difference between the two qualifications concerned, Parties and higher education institutions are, however, encouraged to consider, as far as possible, the merits of the individual qualifications in question without having recourse to an automatic comparison of the length of study required to obtain the qualification. It is the duty of the Party or institution wishing to refuse recognition to show that the differences in question are substantial."[27]

In the case of the medical radiation technologist, it is quite clear that the programme taken in a non-degree granting post-secondary higher education institution should not be an impediment to recognition, because the programme was not taken in a degree granting post-secondary higher education institution. Article VI.1 states that: "Parties should recognize higher education qualifications earned in the higher education system of any other Party unless a substantial difference can be shown between the qualification for which recognition is sought and the corresponding qualification in the country in which recognition is sought. It is underlined that the difference must be both substantial and relevant as defined by the competent recognition authority. Recognition cannot be withheld for reasons immaterial to the qualification or the purpose for which recognition is sought. It is the responsibility of the Party or higher education institution wishing to refuse recognition to show that the difference is substantial."[28]

It seems that, in the case of the medical radiation technologist, recognition should not have been withheld due to the fact that it was taken in a non-degree granting post-secondary higher education institution in North America. The reason given appears "immaterial to the qualification" in the recognition process, given that the medical radiation technologist programmes in North America are not necessarily offered by post-secondary degree granting higher education institutions. Nothing prevents such a programme from being offered in non-degree granting post-secondary higher education institutions. What is important is that the knowledge and the skills certified by the non-degree granting post-secondary higher education

---

27. Article IV.1, Explanatory Report to the Convention on the Recognition of Qualifications concerning Higher Education in the European Region in www.cicic.ca/docs/Lisboa/Explanatory.en.pdf.
28. Article VI.1, Explanatory Report to the Convention on the Recognition of Qualifications concerning Higher Education in the European Region, in www.cicic.ca/docs/Lisboa/Explanatory.en.pdf.

institution are clearly demonstrated and that the competencies of the individual should have been recognised.

Following initial discussions in Tallinn, the ENIC/NARIC networks pursued their deliberations, building upon the opinions and arguments put forth during the 2006 meeting. The concept was also discussed during the annual meetings held in Bucharest in 2007 and Malta in 2008. Throughout these debates, the understanding of the participants varied greatly. Many grappled with the meaning of the concept and quite a few had reservations as to the importance of considering substantial differences during the assessment of credentials. Some were vehement in citing the importance of equivalencies or even strict nostrification of credentials, insisting that a foreign credential had to be in all points identical to a credential in their country. Many looked at the concept with an open mind but had difficulty integrating it in their formal assessment processes.

A few were at ease with the concept and understood the importance of learning outcomes, competencies and a good understanding of the educational systems of the countries in which a credential is earned. They were very much in favour of pursuing in-depth discussions on the concept of substantial differences and its crucial importance. Some questioned the value of taking into account the duration of studies during an assessment process and even wondered if it was still a relevant criterion. Others admitted that learning outcomes is still a vague concept that is far from being implemented everywhere and that a better understanding of educational systems would help in understanding differences. The discussions of the ENIC/NARIC networks in Tallinn and in subsequent meetings confirmed that, to this day, the concept of substantial differences is far from being well mastered.

Conclusion

A shift in attitudes needs to happen if international credential assessments are to facilitate student and labour mobility from one country to another in a globalised world. Barriers must be torn down and assessments should be done by taking into account level of studies commensurate with the qualification, the workload, the experience and the quality of post-secondary higher education programmes. Receiving countries should focus on learning outcomes, competencies, skills and knowledge, as well as the profile and experience of the individual who wishes to integrate into the labour market in a foreign country.

The discussions undertaken in ENIC and NARIC network meetings and in other international forums demonstrate that substantial differences will take time to be understood in a changing global environment. Important changes in country legislation will need to occur if we are to see significant progress in assessment procedures. These laws have not yet been adapted to changing global realities. They are an impediment to the good will of international credential assessors.

Recruitment to health professions: the case of a Master of Arts in Psychological Sciences

Erwin Malfroy

Introduction

As demonstrated elsewhere in this book, the main principle of the Lisbon Recognition Convention is that foreign qualifications shall be recognised unless there is a substantial difference between the foreign qualification for which recognition is sought and the corresponding qualification of the host country. We have also seen that interpretations by credentials evaluators of this key concept vary significantly.

The Lisbon Recognition Convention acknowledges that the burden of proof of a substantial difference lies with the competent recognition authority of the host country. Three accompanying guidelines in the implementation of the recognition of qualifications are:

– every difference should not be considered "substantial";

– the existence of a substantial difference entails no obligation not to recognise the foreign qualification;

– the difference should be substantial in relation to the function of the qualification and the purpose for which recognition is sought.

Taking into account the diversity – which is an added value – of higher education systems, accepting differences between qualifications will increase the academic and professional mobility opportunities of holders of foreign qualifications.

Furthermore, in the European context, it will contribute to the achievement of the European Higher Education Area (EHEA) by 2010, because the envisaged EHEA aims to:

– facilitate mobility of students, graduates and higher education staff;

– prepare students for their future careers and for life as active citizens in democratic societies, and support their personal development;

– offer broad access to high-quality higher education, based on democratic principles and academic freedom.

By focusing only on the five key elements that together make up a qualification (level, workload, quality, profile and learning outcomes) and by only taking into account substantial differences, the credentials evaluators will indeed transform their approach from looking for "equivalence" to granting "recognition" to an attitude of "acceptance".

Case study

Presentation of the case study

Topic of the case study

The human resources manager of a hospital located in country Y wishes to employ a psychologist from country X.

Information regarding the applicant

The information gathered from the ENIC/NARIC centre of country X regarding the higher education qualification in psychology held by the applicant from this country is as follows:

- the qualification is called Master of Arts in Psychological Sciences;
- the issuing institution is a private accredited university college;
- the study load of the master's programme is 60 ECTS credits;
- the master's programme is a professionally oriented training programme;
- the accreditation system in country X is institution-based: the independent Centre of Accreditation and Quality Assurance ensures the quality of teaching and research at the higher education institutions (that is accreditation is of the institution, rather than of each study programme);
- the profession of psychologist is regulated in country X and the applicant has direct access to this regulated profession in his/her country;
- The applicant has five years' relevant professional experience as a psychologist in his/her country.

Information on the similar qualification in country Y

The similar higher education qualification in country Y has the following characteristics:

- the similar qualification is called Master in Psychology;
- the issuing institution is a recognised university;
- the study load of the similar master's programme is 120 ECTS credits;
- the similar master's programme is an academically oriented study programme with lots of strong scientific research components;
- the accreditation system in country Y is programme based: the competent accreditation body independently ensures the quality of higher education by assessing and accrediting programmes (that is, accreditation is for each study programme);
- the profession of psychologist is not regulated in country Y.

Overview

	Country X	Country Y
Qualifications	Master of Arts in Psychological Sciences	Master in Psychology
Issuing institution	Private accredited (recognised) university college	Recognised university
ECTS credits	60 ECTS	120 ECTS
Diploma supplement and additional information	The master's programme is a professionally oriented training programme The accreditation system is institution based	The master's programme is an academically oriented higher education programme The accreditation system is programme based
Additional applicant information	The profession of "psychologist" is regulated and the applicant has direct access to the regulated profession "psychologist" The applicant has five years of relevant professional experience as a psychologist	The profession "psychologist" is not regulated

Discussion

State of affairs

The human resources manager of a hospital located in country Y wishes to employ a psychologist from country X. She has requested advice from the ENIC/NARIC centre in country Y regarding the qualification of the candidate, who holds the degree Master of Arts in Psychological Sciences.

Credential evaluation

Additional information

If you were the credentials evaluator of the ENIC/NARIC centre of country Y, what additional information would you need in order to fairly assess this case?

Academic recognition – substantial difference items

Assuming that the additional information is obtained, what factors would you consider to be:

a.   substantial differences that prevent academic recognition?

b.   differences that do not hinder academic recognition?

Professional recognition – the European directive

If you consider the differences to be substantial, and both countries are members of the European Economic Area, would you be able to use the applicable European legislation (European Directive 2005/36/EC) for professional recognition?

Learning outcomes

What would your decision be if the competent medical authorities in both countries confirm that the learning outcomes of the higher education programme leading to a Master of Arts in Psychological Sciences in country X meet the minimum standards for exercising the profession of psychologist in a hospital in country X and Y?

Remarks and comments by the participants

Additional information

If the psychologist has access to the doctoral programme/training in his/her country X, this element is considered a positive factor in the evaluation of the foreign master's degree.

Since a difference should be both important and relevant to the purpose for which recognition is sought[29] (in this case the purpose for which recognition is sought is employment as a psychologist in a hospital in country Y), additional information regarding the profile and the learning outcomes of the master's programme Master of Arts in Psychological Sciences in country X is desirable and has an additional benefit:

–   the profile: in view of the fact that the purpose for which recognition is sought is exercising the profession of psychologist in a hospital, additional information regarding the professionally oriented aspect of the master's programme will be useful and will be a bonus element for the applicant;

–   the learning outcomes: if the learning outcomes of the master's programme in country X are indeed comparable with the Dublin Descriptors[30] of the second level, this additional information may compensate for possible study load differences.

---

29. In Article VI.1 of the Explanatory Report of the Lisbon Recognition Convention it is underlined that the difference must be both substantial and relevant as defined by the competent recognition authority. Recognition cannot be withheld for reasons immaterial to the qualification or the purpose for which recognition is sought.

30. www.jointquality.nl/content/descriptors/CompletesetDublinDescriptors.doc.

Extra information regarding the bachelor's programme which gives graduates (direct) access to the master's programme – Master of Arts in Psychological Sciences – in country X may also be of added value. For instance, if the bachelor's programme concerned (for example, Bachelor of Honours) has a study load of 240 ECTS credits, the difference in study load between the comparable master's programmes may become only a difference and not a substantial one.

ECTS	Country X	Country Y
Bachelor	240	180
Master	60	120
Total	*300*	*300*

If the native language of country X is not the same as the native language of country Y, a specified and proven level of language skills regarding the language of country Y by the psychologist from country X may be an additional requirement for the human resources manager of the hospital located in country Y, but this is definitely not a factor that might constitute a substantial difference in the assessment of the qualification itself.

Academic recognition – substantial difference items

The difference in the title of the master's degree, Master of Arts in Psychological Sciences and Master in Psychology is not an issue.

The difference between "university" and "university college" is, in this particular case, for most of the evaluating ENIC and NARIC centres, not a substantial one because:

a. the purpose of the recognition concerns employment in a hospital and the professional orientation of the higher education programme concerned is (even) an added value, because it is relevant to the purpose for which recognition is sought;

b. in the explanatory report to the Lisbon Recognition Convention regarding Article VI.1, it is underlined that the difference must be both substantial and relevant to the purpose for which recognition is sought.

The difference in accreditation systems is not substantial because:

a. the learning outcomes are the same and the same minimum quality level of the higher education training in country X is guaranteed;

b. the profession is regulated in country X, so the difference is not substantial in the aspect of the professional competences.

The difference in study load is not substantial because:

a.   in this particular case, the higher education programme leading to the degree Master of Arts in Psychological Sciences is professionally oriented and the applicant's purpose in applying in country X is to exercise his/her profession;

b.   even if argument (a) is not possible or acceptable for the evaluation centre of country Y, the applicant's five years' professional experience may be regarded as a compensation for the difference in study load;

c.   if the bachelor's programme followed by the applicant has a study load of 240 ECTS credits, the difference in study load between the comparable master's programmes is only a difference and not a substantial one.

Professional recognition – the European directive

The current case study

European Economic Area		
Country X		**Country Y**
Psychologist is a regulated profession		Psychologist is not a regulated profession

If the credentials evaluation centre considers the difference to be substantial, and both countries are members of the European Economic Area, it is not possible to use the European legislation for professional recognition (European Directive 2005/36/EC), because the profession of psychologist is not a regulated profession in the host country.

The European Directive 2005/36/EC will be applicable only if the profession of psychologist (or whatever the exact name of that profession is in the host country) is regulated in the host country.

The "vice-versa" case

European Economic Area		
Country X		**Country Y**
Psychologist is not a regulated profession		Psychologist is a regulated profession

If the situation were reversed (the profession of psychologist is regulated in the host country, but not in the country of the applicant), European Directive 2005/36/EC would be applicable.

Since the psychologist from country X has five years' relevant professional experience as a psychologist, which was effectively and lawfully pursued, the professional experience must be taken into account by the host country Y as a compensation measure for the difference in study load and the non-regulated status of the profession of psychologist.

According to European Directive 2005/36/EC[31] access to, and pursuit of, the profession shall always be granted to applicants who have pursued the profession on a full-time basis for two years during the previous 10 years in another member state which does not regulate that profession.

Learning outcomes

"Learning outcomes" are the magic words. All participants agreed, without discussion, on a positive recognition decision if the competent medical authorities in both countries confirm that the learning outcomes of the higher education programme leading to a Master of Arts in Psychological Sciences in country X meet the minimum quality standards for being a psychologist in a hospital in countries X and Y.

Additional suggestions

One of the additional suggestions to help solve this case (and to reassure the holders of the same degree in the host country) was to offer the psychologist from country X a kind of general (not specific) recognition of his/her degree at master's level but with a lower salary as assistant psychologist in the hospital. Of course, this is only lawful and possible in countries where the professions of psychologist and assistant psychologist are not regulated, as is the case in country Y.

If country X is a third country (not a member of the EEA or the EHEA) more detailed information regarding the workload, the profile and the learning outcomes of the preceding bachelor's programme would be very useful in order to get the global higher education training picture of the applicant.

Also, more detailed information regarding the national quality assurance system of country X and the quality status of the awarding higher education institution (the accreditation system in country X is institution-based) is very useful for credentials evaluators in order to be assured that the independent Centre of Accreditation and Quality Assurance has indeed ensured – at the time the applicant studied and graduated – the quality of teaching and research at the awarding private higher education institution.

All the participants agreed that a possible difference in ranking (for example, a significant lower ranking or even a non-ranking by the awarding higher education institution) between the awarding higher education institution and the local higher education institutions may not be regarded as a substantial difference, as it is stipulated in the Lisbon Recognition Convention. The question "What is the added value of ranking for credentials evaluators?" arose.

---

31. Article 13.2 of the European Directive 2005/36/EC stipulates the following: "Access to and pursuit of the profession shall also be granted to applicants who have pursued the profession referred to in that paragraph on a full-time basis for two years during the previous ten years in another Member State which does not regulate that profession, providing they possess one or more attestations of competence or documents providing evidence of formal qualifications."

Conclusion

Since the powers of the ENIC and NARIC centres differ from country to country (from providing information, through issuing advisory statements, to making legally binding decisions), the attitude towards substantial difference is still diverse, but in many centres it has progressively evolved from "equivalence" to "recognition" to "acceptance".

Almost all ENIC and NARIC centres will accept differences in cases where these differences are not substantial and the local definition of "substantial" is constricted enough to permit discretion.

Credentials evaluators ought no longer to be focused on the study load of the foreign higher education programme alone. A difference in ECTS credits alone, for example a difference of 30 or even 60 credits, will no longer necessarily be considered as substantial. Evaluators are also taking into account other elements, like the learning outcomes. Incidentally, the existence of a substantial difference, regarding study load, for example, entails no obligation not to recognise the foreign qualification.

The "access" element also plays an important role in current credentials evaluation.

The fact that the foreign master's degree gives access to further studies, in this case the PhD programme, is a very positive element for the evaluation, since it underscores the academic status of the qualification.

Many ENIC and NARIC centres do not take into account the initial access requirements of the foreign higher education programme, even if they may have done so in the past. The ENIC and NARIC centres do not consider a difference in the access and admission requirements of the applicant's higher education programme and the requirements for the similar programme in the host country as substantial.

The European directive is indeed an alternative recognition tool to tackle differences in the programme components, but the scope is limited. It is, for instance, only applicable for regulated professions and it is only applicable in the full member states of the European Economic Area.

Learning outcomes is *the* recognition tool. All participants agreed on a positive recognition decision if the learning outcomes of the foreign higher education programme are broadly the same as the learning outcomes of the higher education programme in their own country.

A study of substantial differences: professional teaching qualifications

E. Stephen Hunt

One of the increasingly common issues which credentials evaluators have to deal with is the matter of professional qualifications. These qualifications differ from other academic cases in two ways: (1) the degree, diploma or certificate constitutes preparation, in whole or in part, for entry into a licensed profession; and (2) the individual presenting such a qualification usually seeks to practise the profession in the host country. The nature of professional qualifications is thus at once both academic and legal, and requires evaluators to address both its educational content and purpose and the national laws and regulations governing access to professional licensure and work. Access to professional licensure is often far more strictly regulated than admission to higher education studies or general employment. It may also involve the judgment of other authorities, such as professional licensing boards, in addition to the educational recognition authority.

School teaching qualifications were selected as the example in this case, because teaching is, almost without exception, a regulated profession everywhere and because school teachers often seek to move across borders, to undertake temporary or permanent assignments. Temporary assignments may escape some of the national regulation required for permanent positions because of the nature of these jobs (often exchange programmes or supplemental roles under the supervision of licensed teachers, with no permanent job competition implications). Permanent job seekers, of course, are subject to the full licensure requirements of their new home. Both types of work involve analysis of the adequacy of the candidate's preparation for professional work, in the context of the host country's expectations for the teaching profession.

The case example also presents educational issues related to the content and structure of the degree programme in each of the fictitious countries. In country X, there is a first degree of typical length, followed by a professional teaching certificate with relatively little documentation, although the degree is in modern languages – the subject to be taught – and there is a specified practical training programme following the subject degree. In country Y, by comparison, there are more detailed content requirements for the programme, including specified academic and practical experience standards, and the programme consists of a single first degree involving a slightly greater number of credits than both the degree and certificate for country X. Neither country's programmes appear to include a Diploma Supplement or similar document.

The professional teaching qualifications case was prepared for the 15th Joint Meeting of the ENIC and NARIC networks in Qawra, Malta and presented on 16 June 2008. The participants, from a total of 50 national centres, were divided into four groups and this case, along with several others, was presented sequentially to the four groups. Once the case was presented, participants had an opportunity to discuss the case and provide reactions. Notes were taken that provide the basis of the analysis below.

The presentation fact pattern for the case was as follows.

Case study

The recognition centre in country X has been approached by the head of a state secondary school in their country, who wishes to appoint a modern foreign languages teacher from country Y. Official recognition of a teacher's qualifications is required in order to obtain a work permit in country X.

	Country X	**Country Y**
Qualification(s) required to teach foreign languages to secondary school exit level	Bachelor's degree in Modern Languages and post-graduate Certificate of Education	Bachelor's degree in Modern Foreign Languages and Education
Credits	180+60	280
Graduate learning outcomes described in the Diploma Supplement	No Diploma Supplement issued	"Language component: Graduates are able to communicate fluently and effectively both orally and in writing in two of the languages offered on the program (French, Spanish, English, Italian, German); they have a solid contextual understanding of the language skills acquired (historical, geographical, political and social) and are able to formulate reasoned opinions and substantive arguments in the relevant languages

	Country X	Country Y
		Education component: Graduates are fully prepared to be effective teachers of modern languages from beginners through to advanced secondary school exit level; they are competent practitioners of modern teaching methods, learning pedagogy, differentiation, assessment practices and ICTs in the classroom. As a result of their in-course teaching practice, graduates have the necessary classroom management skills to function at both the national and international levels and in multi-cultural teaching and learning environments".

Discussion questions

1. If you were the credentials evaluator of country X, what additional information would you need in order to assess this case fairly?

2. Assuming that the additional information is obtained, would you recognise the applicant's qualification from country Y? Which elements would you consider to be (a) substantial differences that prevent recognition and (b) differences that do not hinder recognition?

3. If you were the credentials evaluator in country X, who due to existing legislation was forced to give a negative request for recognition, what steps would you take to raise your concerns about the restrictive nature of the current legislation?

4. As a non-recognition expert, do you consider there to be substantial differences between the requirements to teach foreign languages in country X and country Y? Why/Why not?

Results of the discussion

Some participants actively discussed the case, while others did not. Of the 50 total participating countries, persons representing 27 countries, or 54%, provided responses that were clear and usable. In the discussion, issues related to each discussion question will be addressed in turn, followed by the probable recognition outcome.

The need for more information

Several participants stated that it would be helpful to have additional information, specifically evidence of practical experience, evidence of subject specificity, evidence that the applicant from country Y possessed a current and valid teaching licence, or evidence that the programme was quality assured by a recognised competent authority in country Y. The breakdown of those requesting additional information was:

Practicum or proof of experience	7
Subject specificity	5
Valid teaching licence/work permit	6
Status as an EU country citizen	1
Recognised accreditation/QA	1
Diploma Supplement	1
Total requesting more information	21

It was immediately clear during the discussion that professional documentation and work issues were going to be more important than academic issues in this case. Fourteen participants, or 67% of those who asked for more information stated that they needed documentation of the country Y candidate's work experience, licensure, and – in one case – even his or her citizenship. Of the seven respondents who asked for educational information, one sought information on the status of the institution, one stated the need for a Diploma Supplement and, of the other five, "subject specificity" usually meant that one of the languages for the country Y degree needed to be the national language of their country.

Providing requested additional information

It appeared that most of the respondents needing more information would, or might, give positive consideration to the country Y candidate if the requested documentation could be provided. Three respondents indicated that they could not grant or recommend full recognition regardless of additional information. One gave no reason; another could only recognise the qualification for teaching in language schools rather than regular public schools; while a third did not recognise the subject "modern foreign languages" as valid and in any case required a master's degree for language teachers rather than a bachelor's.

Raising concerns about restrictive regulations

The discussion demonstrated that most of the responding participants who needed information or had doubts about the qualification from country Y (and some for country X as well) were labouring under quite strict professional licensure requirements. The issue was not usually whether respondents thought that the degree structure or quality was in question, but rather whether the applicant could meet strict regulations governing work experience and documentation. Academic preparation

– except for mastering the national language in some cases – was not at issue, and many thought that the graduate from country Y was probably prepared to teach from an educational standpoint. Having the papers and the professional apprenticeship time (internships, practical or actual work) was another matter. Both documentation (Diploma Supplement, teaching licence, work permit, licensure examinations, citizenship) and practical experience (actual numbers of hours worked) were based in rigid statutory or regulatory language and gave little or no room for discretion.

The situation is not uncommon in professional mobility. Most countries try, through legislation or licensing board requirements, to restrict access to regulated professions due to labour, economic or other reasons. Cross-border professional mobility is even more restricted, due to the capacity to absorb foreign workers, protectionism, and efforts to ensure that workers are trained to a standard comparable to that of domestic professionals. Such a situation is complicated in Europe because of the recent emergence of the European Union, which posits increased mobility among member states and programmes of outreach to attract and regulate immigration and temporary mobility from non-members. In addition, the various European treaties regulate professions and work differently, depending on whether responsibility rests with the European Commission directorates or with national authorities. In the specific case of teaching, responsibility remains with national authorities, but with pressures created by mechanisms to promote intra-European mobility.

The participants in the case discussion were largely silent as to whether they could or would attempt to influence national policy makers with respect to moderating restrictive regulations. The representatives of two countries pointed out that the decision-making responsibility for professional recognition of teachers lay outside the control of credentials evaluators. National teaching boards made such determinations and only relied on the ENIC or NARIC for advice concerning the educational backgrounds of applicants. Others were constrained by statutes that could only be modified by legislative action. In most cases, the ENICs, NARICs and other credentials evaluation authorities are either members of the civil service, government contractors or private citizens. Their capacity to influence national policy is often limited by legal constraints, ethical conflict of interest issues, and the power of small, specialised technical service providers to attract the attention of the powerful.

Substantial difference concerns

There were three main issues touching upon substantial difference that concerned the participants: (1) whether the modern languages studied included the national teaching language of the country in which work was being sought; (2) whether the course of study incorporated adequate pre-licensure teaching experiences such as supervised practical; and (3) whether the programme or awarding institution was accredited. It was noteworthy that not a single participant referred to the relative length, number of credits, or sequence structure of the qualifications. The fact that both qualifications involved a first degree was sufficient in all cases, except for one country, where a master's degree was required for language teachers.

Given the efforts put into promoting the recognition concepts of the Lisbon convention, it was salutary to realise that – from an educational standpoint – the potential substantial difference issues in this case involved genuine questions of academic subject content and accreditation. The level and purpose of both the country X and country Y qualifications were broadly accepted as comparable, and no "bean-counting" issues such as credit counts or years reared their heads.

"Bean-counting" issues did, of course, emerge when the issue became reconciling specific licensure requirements. Some respondents noted that both qualifications seemed to include practical training, but nevertheless could not grant recognition unless there was proof that a specified number of teaching hours had been achieved. Others had to have specific types of documentation or approvals. A good argument could be made that some licensure requirements, such as possessing a valid current teaching licence in the home country, are universally legitimate and the basis of a substantial difference concern. Likewise, the requirement that a graduate of a teacher-training programme have substantial practical training, as well as academic preparation, is probably universally desirable given the nature of the teaching profession. Given the wide variety of programmes in the world, including high-quality programmes, it is perhaps not so wise to impose inflexible rules on the precise number of practice hours any more than credits or length – at least not if one intends to promote international mobility.

Requiring documentation also has pitfalls as well as advantages. Possessing a currently valid licence may be considered a valid expectation and a professional substantial difference if it does not exist. Even if the lack of a licence is through no fault of the applicant, it could well mean that they either have been out of the profession for a long time, or have taught in substandard or unaccredited schools, either of which would be legitimate grounds for concern. Requesting clear documentation of the level, type, purpose and status of the qualification – such as a Diploma Supplement – can also be considered a legitimate expectation. While a Diploma Supplement may be the choice within Europe (and a cause for concern that only one respondent required it), this may not, however, be something to rigidly impose on non-European applicants. It may be sufficient to require equivalent transparent information such as a transcript, proof of recognised accreditation, for example. Imposing the Diploma Supplement universally, while not admitting legitimate counterparts, could be construed as protectionism rather than quality control; likewise the issue of work permits or citizenship. It is next to impossible to obtain a work permit, or even a work visa, without first undergoing a credentials evaluation. To require a work permit first effectively puts the cart before the horse and could be interpreted as a clear effort to keep out foreign – or foreign-educated – professionals. As to citizenship, it is hard to understand how national policies can realistically recognise – much less attract – internationally mobile professionals if the first requirement be that the applicant is either a citizen of the country or of another EU member state.

Overall recognition recommendations

Based on the foregoing discussion, it is perhaps worthwhile to state what the recognition outcome would be, based on the case fact pattern. Assuming the recognition analysis had to make do with what was presented in the case, with no additional information, the participants reacted as follows:

Yes: probable full recognition of the qualification	11 (40.7%)
Partial recognition of various types	5 (18.5%)
No: recognition could not be expected	11 (40.7%)

The majority of those who said no based their conclusion on the lack of proof of sufficient practical teaching hours, lack of evidence that the national language is required, or lack of proof of a teaching licence. For those who could recommend partial recognition, the primary issues needing resolution were, again, insufficient practical training and the need to complete the national licensure examination sequence of the host country, regardless of prior licences. Those disposed to partial recognition generally believed that full recognition could be granted if these additional steps were fulfilled.

Conclusion

There is no question but that the recognition of teaching qualifications, and most likely other qualifications to practice licensed professions, does not depend so much on academic considerations as on professional licensing requirements. It is the rules governing work documentation, practical work experience, licensing examinations, and other legal requirements that drive the decision and that often permit very little flexibility on the part of a credentials evaluator. The credential – qualification – itself is not an issue unless, its content (such as the national language or practical), level (bachelor's versus higher degree), or purpose presents a problem.

In this particular case, the level, purpose and content of the fictitious qualifications were not at issue, except in a few situations where individual countries required a different degree level, or a more explicit content description. What was at issue was whether the applicant had a license or permit, proof of the legitimacy of the qualification, work experience of a requisite period of time, or had undertaken other steps, such as the host country examination process. Some of these requirements, such as an existing license, competence in the language of instruction, adequate practical experience, and graduation from a quality-assured programme can properly be considered substantive questions, with a question of a substantial difference arising if they are not met. Many of the others are process questions, having procedural rather than substantive importance, and so the question of their necessity – and whether they are sufficiently flexible – must needs arise. Since these matters are usually the prerogative of national authorities other than credentials evaluators, and often on a higher political level, where economic and other non-educational considerations prevail, there is no easy way to make such rules more friendly to international mobility and recognition.

An example of professional recognition: social work

Françoise Profit and Jean-Philippe Restoueix

In this fictitious example, the holder of a qualification from country Y contacts a credentials evaluator in country X, with a view to being employed as a social worker in country X.

	Country X	Country Y
Qualifications required for social workers	University diploma plus two years of professional activity as social worker with a public authority	*"Licence"* degree in social work
Degree granting institution	A recognised university	Institute for Social Work
ECTS credits required	300	240
Supplementary information concerning the Diploma Supplement	The degree course emphasises solid theoretical and practical knowledge and understanding in sociology	The qualification builds on theoretical training, as well as a traineeship or other experience outside the classroom as an integral part of the study programme; students devote 50% of their study time to practical work
Other documents provided by the candidate	–	Attestation of traineeships certifying the work undertaken in several recognised social services in country Y

The discussion in the networks focused on the following elements:

a. The first question concerns the purpose of the recognition sought. In this case, the purpose is professional recognition and, in some countries, the profession of "social workers" is regulated. The recognition might have been considered differently had the purpose been recognition with a view to pursuing further academic studies.

b. The term "social worker" describes realities that differ quite a bit from one country to another. Depending on the country, the term "social worker" may describe a range of professions from paramedics to special educators, from civil servants in charge of controlling a number of social programmes to professionals in charge of direct assistance to certain disadvantaged groups. It is therefore essential to have a good understanding of the reality of the profession in country Y and to see to what extent this is also true for country X.

c.   In addition, the fact that "social work" is often a regulated profession in EU countries raises the issue of whether there is a substantial difference if country Y is a non-EU country. If so, professional recognition will not be accorded automatically under European Directive 2005/36/EC. In this sense, it seems important to extend the discussion on recognition to a broader consideration of diplomas and qualifications and to include also qualifications issues in non-EU countries.

d.   In the case covered by this study, it is also important to obtain as much information as possible on the status and study programme(s) of the Institute for Social Work, in particular with a view to determining:

- the balance between academic and practical training;

- possibilities of employment, as well as of continued academic studies, on the basis of the qualification issued by this institute in the country of origin.

It is also necessary to verify how professional experience is validated in country X, and in particular to see whether there is a system of recognition of practical experience that could take account of all the practical experience included in the study programme in country Y.

e.   As a final point, the difference between the credits obtained in country X and those required in country Y could prove to be of little importance if the purpose of the application is professional recognition, since the number of credits are not taken account of in professional recognition.

Survey on substantial differences: an example of practice in Europe

Bas Wegewijs

Introduction: recapitulation of the case

In 2008, one of the NARIC projects funded by the European Commission within the Lifelong Learning Programme was the Survey on Substantial Differences, carried out by a project team consisting of the NARICs of the Netherlands (NUFFIC), the United Kingdom, Norway and Lithuania. The project was based on the findings of the Working Party on Substantial Differences, and aimed to provide an overview of daily practice in dealing with substantial differences within the NARIC Network. The results of the survey are described in another article ("Substantial differences in an EU context: conclusions from a project") in this volume.

During the course of the project, it was agreed with the Working Party on Substantial Differences that it would be worthwhile to include one of the cases of the survey in the workshops to be held at the annual joint meeting of the ENIC and NARIC networks. The selected case represented one of the main issues of the survey: to what extent do the formal rights of a qualification determine the outcome of the evaluation, and to what extent are learning outcomes taken into account? The case involved the simple situation of a student seeking admission to a master's programme on the basis of a bachelor's degree. The possible substantial difference in formal rights was that this particular bachelor's degree did not give access to master's programmes in the home country. Such a situation exists in educational systems where the one-year bachelor's honours programme is an intermediate step between the bachelor's and master's programmes. As an example, a Bachelor of Arts in Historical Studies from South Africa was chosen. The basic question then is: do we base the whole of our evaluation on the fact that this degree does not give access to the master's programme in South Africa (leading to the outcome: recognition denied, since the qualification does not give access in the home country), or do we still try to establish whether the learning outcomes would be sufficient to enrol in the master's programme? In the latter case, the outcome of the evaluation might still be negative (no access to master's programme, because of substantial differences in learning outcomes, for example limited scope for independent study and research), but not for formal reasons. The result of the evaluation might also be positive (access to master's programme if the learning outcomes meet the requirements of the host country), in which case the substantial difference in formal rights of the qualification is effectively ignored.

On 16 June 2008, the case was presented to the ENIC and NARIC networks four times in a row, to four different groups of approximately 20-25 participants, in sessions of 30 minutes. Following the format shown below, participants were asked to choose their preferred option, to provide alternative options if relevant and to rate all of the options provided. After noting down all of the scores, participants were invited to discuss the various options for the remainder of the workshop.

In the present article, the results of the various scores are presented and the outcome of the discussions is summarised, leading to some conclusions on this particular question of substantial difference.

Case study as presented to participants of the workshops

CASE 1	
Country of origin	South Africa
Qualification	Bachelor of Arts in Historical Studies
Purpose of evaluation	Admission to master's programme in history
Possible substantial difference	Qualification does not give access to master's programmes in South Africa (a bachelor's honours degree is required)

1. How would your office evaluate this qualification?

☐ **A** – No access to master's programme (since the qualification does not give access in the home country)

☐ **B** – No access to master's programme, because of substantial differences in learning outcomes (for example, limited scope for independent study and research)

☐ **C** – Access to master's programme if the learning outcomes meet the requirements of the host country

☐ **D** – Other:

2. How do you rate the options given above in view of the Lisbon Recognition Convention?

	Best practice	Good practice	Acceptable practice	Unacceptable practice
Option A	☐	☐	☐	☐
Option B	☐	☐	☐	☐
Option C	☐	☐	☐	☐
(Option D)	☐	☐	☐	☐

3. Do you have any further comments on this specific substantial difference?

Results: discussions within the working groups

Initial discussions

In all four working groups there was some initial discussion on the way the case was stated. Furthermore, questions were asked in order to clarify the case.

Some of the main issues were as follows:

1. More information was required to evaluate the case. Some participants insisted that no attempt at all could be made to do an evaluation without having seen a list of subjects taken, credits awarded and grades obtained. In answer to this objection, it was pointed out that the absence of such detailed information was intentional: participants were required to take one step backward and to evaluate the case from broad principles. Furthermore, by looking at the phrasing of the options, it is clear that it is not always necessary to know the exact outcome of the evaluation in order to choose between the options.

2. Some participants remarked that the options provided were not all inclusive, or that two of the options could be interpreted as representing two sides of the same coin. With respect to option B, it was mentioned that this option supposes that the evaluation always leads to the outcome that there are substantial differences. As participants felt that they were not prepared to draw that conclusion without having seen more details of the programme, option B was not chosen by any of the participants. In answer to these comments, it was suggested that participants could provide their own alternative options under option D. Furthermore, participants were referred to the rating system in order to express their opinions on the acceptability of the options, even if they were not prepared to choose certain options.

3. It was pointed out by one or two participants that exceptions exist to the basic assumption that in South Africa a bachelor's degree is not sufficient to be admitted to a master's programme (and that a bachelor's honours degree is required). In answer to this objection, participants were asked to consider the case to be an example of the situation where there is no possibility of entering the master's programme, and to continue with the evaluation on that basis.

4. One participant mentioned that, according to the procedure of his office, the outcome of the evaluation would depend on the nationality of the holder of the qualification (EU citizen or not), information that was not provided in the description of the case. After some heated debate among participants, who seemed to challenge the validity of this particular procedure, the participant was advised to evaluate the case assuming that the diploma holder was not an EU citizen.

After having clarified and discussed these issues, participants were asked to join in the evaluation session as best they could, under the circumstances.

Results of the evaluations and ratings

The participants were asked to vote for the various options and ratings by raising their hands. Although not all participants voted on all questions raised, the resulting scores seem to provide a good overview of the attitudes and opinions of the workshop participants.

Table of evaluation and ratings results (scores are given in percentages)

CASE 1 – South African bachelor's degree	Score	Best practice	Good practice	Acceptable practice	Unacceptable practice
A No access to master's programme (since the qualification does not give access in the home country)	38.6	10.4	9.0	56.7	23.9
B No access to master's programme, because of substantial differences in learning outcomes (for example, limited scope for independent study and research)	0	0	34.0	62.0	4.0
C Access to master's programme if the learning outcomes meet the requirements of the host country	52.9	50.8	27.7	18.5	3.1
D Other	8.6				

In the table above, all of the scores for the various options and the ratings of the options are collected, taking into account the voting of all four workshop sessions.

The votes for the open option D (other) were divided between the two following outcomes:

- no direct access to the master's programme, but to a bridging course leading to the master's programme;

- conditional access to the master's programme, implying that some specific requirements should be fulfilled by the student during the course of the master's programme.

These two additional options in terms of partial recognition and conditional recognition might effectively be regarded as belonging to option B, if we would formulate this option as "no full or direct access to master's programme, because of substantial differences in learning outcomes".

Even if we were to add the votes for option D to the score of option B, it is clear that only a very small minority preferred option B. The results show that option C and A are most popular among the participants, with option C as the winning option (53%). This is in contrast to the outcome of the NARIC survey (see the accompanying article in this volume), where A was the winning option. However, both the survey and the workshop results showed a clear preference for option C as representing best practice.

Discussion of the voting and the rating

On the basis of the results of the voting, participants were asked to comment on their vote. Special attention was given to participants who came up with an extra option on how to deal with the qualification; each of them was asked to provide a short description and explanation of their option. Also, participants who took opposite views on a certain option (for instance by rating that option as "best practice" and "unacceptable practice" respectively) were asked to discuss their reasons for arriving at that conclusion.

In a few instances, participants pointed out that the option they had chosen as being in line with daily practice in their office was not the option they rated highest in terms of good practice. In most cases, this was the case when they rated the option that took into account the learning outcomes of the qualification as best practice. Indeed, this tendency is also clearly reflected in the outcomes of the ratings (see table above).

Various reasons were given for preferring the learning outcomes option, but not following it in daily practice: national law standing in the way, overruling agreements with higher education institutions, a lack of information on learning outcomes to base evaluations on, or a lack of methodology to evaluate learning outcomes.

Some specific comments on future policy were also given:

– At present, our office is bound by law to choose option A, but a change of law is expected, which will give us the opportunity to switch to option C (which we consider to be best practice) in the near future.

– Our office would strongly prefer to base our evaluations on learning outcomes, but we have to wait until suitable methodology has been developed.

Interestingly, in the discussions between participants taking opposite views on the importance of taking into account the formal rights of the qualification in the sending country, no consensus was reached between the two parties. On the contrary, defenders of the two views appeared to be strongly convinced of their opinion, referring to the Lisbon Recognition Convention to back up their arguments and warning each other about the possibility of discrimination.

In general, the two lines of reasoning went as follows:

1. We have to follow the judgment of the South African authorities in their ruling that this particular qualification does not give the right to enter the master's programme. Who are we as a foreign recognition office not to respect this rule? We would clearly offend the South African authorities in admitting such students to our master's programmes, by ignoring their judgment. Furthermore, we would run the risk of giving the impression that our master's programmes are at a lower level than those in South Africa, which could ultimately lead to a devaluation of the standing of our national higher education system. Also, we may be doing the student a disservice, as the master's degree obtained in our country might not be recognised in South Africa, or other countries, in view of the entrance requirements not having been fulfilled. Finally, we would be discriminating against our own national students who do not have the right to enter a master's programme, by admitting foreign students without this same right.

2. If a student fulfils the basic requirements for access to a master's programme and has the competencies to successfully follow the programme, why should we care what the formal rights in the sending country are? The main thing is that we select suitable students with a qualification of good quality, and the South African bachelor's degree may be sufficient for that purpose. Furthermore, the formal rights of a qualification may have to do with the peculiarities of a higher education system, which may have little relevance in our own system. In this case, the South African higher education cycles may be considered to be 3 + 1 + 1 years (bachelor's + bachelor's honours + master's), which may be compared to the European 3 + 2 (bachelor's + master's) cycles. In that case, the formal right to enter the master's programme in South Africa has a different implication than it would have in most European countries. In any case, if we were not to allow the holder of a South African bachelor's degree entrance to our master's programme, although he has achieved similar learning outcomes to our national students, we would be discriminating against him.

Conclusions: some comments on the case and the discussions

The selected case, being based on a clearly identified existing qualification, led to a lively debate among participants, who on the whole appeared to be quite knowledgeable about the topic of substantial differences.

As explained above, there was a clear tendency to go from option A to option C, and not the other way around. That is, no participants that chose option C indicated that option A was actually their preference, but this did happen the other way around. This suggests that option C is the desirable situation, and we might expect option A to be phased out gradually, as more and more countries are likely to give more weight to learning outcomes, as opposed to the formal rights of a qualification.

As such, the case proved to be highly successful in uncovering these underlying differences in applying and weighing formal, national and practical arguments when determining whether fair recognition is being granted. We suggest that the recognition networks should make an effort to achieve more agreement on what is good practice in establishing substantial differences, possibly based on real-life cases such as the ones used in the Survey on Substantial Differences and in the workshops described here.

III. Substantial differences
in a world context

Substantial differences in an EU context: conclusions from a project

Bas Wegewijs and Lucie de Bruin

Introduction

With the adoption of the Lisbon Recognition Convention in 1997, a powerful instrument for providing fair and unbiased recognition was established. However, one of the basic principles of the convention – that one should recognise foreign qualifications unless one can demonstrate there are substantial differences between these foreign qualifications and the corresponding qualifications in one's own system – appears to be quite a challenge in the actual application of the convention. Ever since the adoption of the convention, ENIC/NARIC offices and recognition authorities have been struggling to distinguish between differences and substantial differences (as can be gathered from the present volume).

In response to the initiatives of the ENIC/NARIC Working Party on Substantial Differences, a NARIC project entitled Survey on Substantial Differences was launched in 2007 in order to investigate how the various ENIC/NARIC centres interpret and apply the concept of substantial differences in real-life cases. The project team consisted of the NARICs of the Netherlands (NUFFIC, project co-ordinator), the United Kingdom, Lithuania and Norway.

The one year project started with desktop research on earlier work in this field, including that of the ENIC/NARIC Working Party on Substantial Differences, to establish the framework of the project. Next, each of the four NARICs of the project team collected a set of real-life cases, stemming from their daily practice in credentials evaluation. After having consulted the Working Party on Substantial Differences in April 2008, a selection of 10 real-life cases was made, addressing a variety of possible substantial differences. All of these cases were evaluated by the project team, according to a standard evaluation form. From the results of these evaluations a survey was derived, which was circulated to all members of the NARIC Network in early May 2008.

The survey allowed all of the NARICs to indicate how the 10 particular cases are treated in their office and also to rate the various alternative solutions given in terms of good practice. It was expected that the results of the survey would provide the NARIC Network with a clear overview of how substantial differences are dealt with in actual practice. Such an overview might be helpful for each of the NARIC offices in finding solutions for difficult recognition issues, by learning from the experience of other NARICs. Furthermore, the rating of the various options by all NARICs was expected to provide a picture of where we stand with our daily practice, as seen through the eyes of our peers.

In order not to over-complicate the survey, the descriptions of the qualifications were kept to a minimum. The respondents were expected to fill in the gaps themselves, based on their experience as credentials evaluators. In addition, respondents were requested to answer all the questions, in order to avoid unhelpful statements such as "this is not our decision", which would not enrich the survey results.

All of the cases followed the same basic format. The first question in each case asked the respondents to indicate how the particular case is dealt with in their daily practice. Respondents could choose one of the options provided, or describe an alternative option if none of the other options would fit. The second question in each case provided the opportunity to rate each of the options in terms of acceptability: best practice, good practice, acceptable practice or unacceptable practice. Here, the respondents were asked to take one step backward from daily practice and their own national situation and judge the various options from a general point of view. Finally, a third (open) question provided the chance to express any comments on the particular case and possible substantial differences, either from a national or general point of view.

The descriptions of the 10 cases and the options provided in the survey can be found in the tables in the results section (below).

Results of the survey

The survey was completed by a total of 15 NARIC centres, out of a possible 32 NARICs to which the web survey was sent. This constitutes a response rate of 47%, reflecting the high level of interest within the NARIC Network in the topic of substantial differences. Also, the project was well publicised at network meetings, and the user-friendly web format may have also been helpful in achieving a relatively high response rate. A good regional spread all across Europe was achieved, and the participating countries represent a healthy variation in educational systems and recognition procedures. Furthermore, five of the largest EU countries are represented in the survey. Therefore, we consider the outcomes of this survey to be representative of actual recognition practices within the NARIC Network.

The cases are analysed in terms of the scores obtained by the various options (representing the daily recognition practice of the NARIC offices), and the ratings of the options in terms of good practice. Special attention is given to the overall outcome of the scores: do NARICs more or less agree on what is the best option?

If that is the case, the recognition practice in that particular case is considered to be "convergent". If the opposite options (the most strict one and the most lenient one) both attract a relatively high number of votes, the case is considered to be "controversial".

The open-ended option for each case, in which an alternative approach could be described by the respondent, was not chosen very often. In some cases, it was used to indicate that two of the options provided were both relevant in certain situations, or that no option could be chosen because of lack of information, or that the decision was not in the hands of the NARIC office. As described above, the survey introduction emphasised the need to avoid using this excuse, or a statement such as "this is not our decision", but to evaluate the qualification based on the information available and the recognition practices followed by that NARIC. In other cases, the additional option was used to add some extra comment or reasoning to an option already provided in the survey. Only a few additional options actually described alternative practice in recognition. For reasons of clarity and simplicity, none of the "votes" for the additional options have been taken into account in the analysis below, although the scores for these options appear in the results tables.

Analysis of the cases

Case 1

CASE 1	
Country of origin	South Africa
Qualification	Bachelor of Arts in Historical Studies
Purpose of evaluation	Admission to master's programme in History
Possible substantial difference	Qualification does not give access to master's programmes in South Africa (a bachelor's honours degree is required)

This case was selected to find out to what extent the formal rights attached to a qualification are considered to be a substantial difference, even though the learning outcomes might be similar to those required in the receiving country.

Option A expresses the view that the formal rights in the sending country (no access to the master's programme) determine the outcome of the evaluation: no access to the master's programme in the receiving country. Option B also results in a negative decision, but based on learning outcomes rather than on formal rights. Option C takes the view that access is possible if the learning outcomes meet the requirements, despite the fact that access would not be granted in the sending country.

CASE 1	Score	Best	Good	Acceptable	Unacceptable
A No access to master's programme (since the qualification does not give access in the home country)	**53.3**	20.0	26.7	33.3	20.0
B No access to master's programme, because of substantial differences in learning outcomes (for example limited scope for independent study and research)	13.3	6.7	46.7	46.7	0.0
C Access to master's pro-gramme if the learning outcomes meet the require-ments of the host country	26.7	40.0	26.7	20.0	13.3
D Other	6.7				

The results show that the formal option A is practised by the majority of NARICs (53%), option B is least current (13%) and option C is practised by a quarter of NARICs (27%). This means that there is hardly any middle ground in the opinions, as the two extreme practices are most current. This is a clear example of non-convergent recognition practice in Europe.

Remarkably, option A, though most current, is not considered to be best practice by most NARICs (only 20%), as this honour is awarded to option C (rated by 40% of NARICS as best practice). This becomes even clearer if we combine the percentages for A as best and good practice (47%), which is lower than the percentage of NARICs indicating option A as their own practice. This shows that some of the NARICs currently following option A must be bound to follow this practice, whereas they would rather follow option C. Also, option A is considered to be the most unacceptable option by a fifth of the NARICs, a clear indication of the controversy surrounding this case. Finally, the middle option B does not raise much debate, being rated as good/acceptable practice by the majority of NARICs.

This case was also presented in a workshop on substantial differences at the 2008 joint ENIC/NARIC meeting in Malta. Although the main outcome was different (with option C beating option A), the subsequent discussions among participants revealed the underlying arguments for choosing and rating the various options (see: "Survey on substantial differences: an example of practice in Europe" in this volume).

Case 2

CASE 2	
Country of origin	Spain
Qualification	Master – *título propio* (awarded by a recognised Spanish higher education institution)
Purpose of evaluation	Admission to a doctoral programme
Possible substantial difference	This is not a national Spanish degree

This case raises the issue of degrees awarded by recognised institutions which do not belong to the national degree structure. Should this be considered a substantial difference? The underlying problem is that such programmes usually have a variety of purposes and learning outcomes, which are difficult to link to national standards.

Option A takes the formal stance: no access to the doctoral programme, as it is not a national degree. Option B also results in a negative decision, but leaves the possibility that partial recognition at master's level may be granted. Option C states that admission is possible if the learning outcomes meet the requirements.

CASE 2	Score	Best	Good	Acceptable	Unacceptable
A No access to the doctoral programme (since the qualification is not a national degree)	46.7	20.0	26.7	40.0	13.3
B No access to the doctoral programme, but the qualification will be evaluated and credit may be given to individual subjects/modules	33.3	20.0	26.7	46.7	6.7
C Access to the doctoral programme if the learning outcomes meet the requirements of the host country	6.7	13.3	13.3	46.7	26.7
D Other	13.3				

Again, as in Case 1, the formal argument wins out, being the favoured current practice in almost half of the NARICs. In this case, however, the other extreme (access is possible) is not currently practised very often, while option B (partial recognition) scores quite respectably (33%). Clearly, there is much less controversy in this case, as most NARICs seem to consider that a "genuine" national master's degree is required for entrance into a doctoral programme. This is confirmed by the fact that option C attracts the highest score (more than a quarter of votes) on being unacceptable practice and the lowest on best practice. In all, this is an example of more convergent recognition practice in Europe.

Case 3

CASE 3	
Country of origin	Russian Federation
Qualification	*Kandidat Nauk* (three-year programme), combined with a *Diplom Spetsialist* (five-year programme)
Purpose of evaluation	Comparability with doctoral degree in the host country
Possible substantial difference	Entry requirements for the *Diplom Spetsialist* programme are relatively low compared with the situation in most other European countries.

A substantial difference may occur in the programme(s) preceding the qualification to be evaluated, but how far back is it reasonable to go? This is tested by the case of the Russian *Kandidat Nauk* degree, which builds on a five-year university programme, the entry requirements for which might be considered to be lower than those of the average European university programme, mainly due to the shorter secondary school programme in Russia.

Option A states that despite this difference, the *Kandidat Nauk* degree is fully recognised in the receiving country. Option B takes a stricter view, resulting in only partial recognition at doctoral level. In Option C, the doctoral degree is recognised by default, as no strict criteria exist in the receiving country to make a meaningful comparison.

CASE 3	Score	Best	Good	Acceptable	Unacceptable
A Fully comparable to the doctoral degree of the host country	**60.0**	40.0	26.7	33.3	0.0
B Not comparable to the doctoral degree of the host country (because of the entry requirements of the *Diplom Spetsialist* programme), partial recognition at doctoral level	20.0	0.0	6.7	46.7	46.7

CASE 3	Score	Best	Good	Acceptable	Unacceptable
C Broadly comparable to the doctoral degree of the host country (because of lack of strict requirements for doctoral degree in the host country)	6.7	0.0	20.0	66.7	13.3
D Other	13.3				

The results show that the majority of NARICs do not view this case as representing a major substantial difference. Option A was chosen by 60%, has the highest score for best practice, and a zero score for unacceptable practice. Option B (only partial recognition) comes second, with 20% indicating this as their current practice, but obtains a high score on unacceptability (47%), and scores only 7% on best and good practice combined, much less than the 20% score of the option as current practice. Option C is least popular, but does not involve much controversy (it is merely seen as "acceptable" by the majority). In all, the less strict point of view wins out, with a tendency to go from option B to option A (as expressed by the ratings).

Case 4

CASE 4	
Country of origin	United Kingdom
Qualification	Master's degree (12-month programme)
Purpose of evaluation	Comparability with a master's degree (two-year programme) in the host country
Possible substantial difference	Duration and/or workload

This is a classic case, involving a difference in duration or workload, which has been much debated for many years in the recognition networks.

Option A states that the difference of one year is in itself enough to deny recognition, whereas option B uses the argument of workload to reach the same conclusion. Option C sees no problem with recognition, as long as the learning outcomes are sufficient, while option D uses the formal argument that the rights of the qualification in the sending country should prevail and lead to a positive recognition decision.

CASE 4	Score	Best	Good	Acceptable	Unacceptable
A Not comparable, as the duration of the United Kingdom programme is one year shorter, which is a substantial difference	14.3	7.1	14.3	21.4	57.1
B Not comparable, because of substantial differences in workload	14.3	14.3	7.1	50.0	28.6
C Comparable if the learning outcomes meet the requirements of the host country	28.6	35.7	50.0	14.3	0.0
D Comparable, because the qualification gives access to PhD studies in the United Kingdom	**42.9**	21.4	57.1	21.4	0.0
E Other	0.0				

The clear preference in terms of current practice is option D (43%), followed by C, while A and B come jointly last. Thus, the overall result is that most NARICs would give recognition to this degree, although over a quarter of the NARICs who replied appear to deny recognition of this UK master's degree on the basis of the duration/workload argument. The duration argument is viewed as unacceptable by the majority of NARICs (57%), while the workload argument is somewhat more respectable (29% unacceptable). Both positive options (C and D) are acceptable (or better) for all respondents. Interestingly, the option in terms of learning outcomes (C) has the highest rating on best practice, beating option D, which is, however, the prevailing current practice. Once again, this seems a clear indication of NARICs wishing to move away from the formal duration-based argument to the learning outcomes approach.

Case 5

CASE 5	
Country of origin	The Netherlands
Qualification	Bachelor in Social Work (awarded by a *hogeschool*, university of applied science)

CASE 5	
Purpose of evaluation	Admission to research-based master's programme in social sciences
Possible substantial difference	Contents and profile (possible lack of academic training and research skills)

This case illustrates the possible substantial difference between bachelor's degree programmes that prepare for research and those that are more professionally oriented. Option A states that no access to a research-based master's programme is possible, on the basis of a professionally oriented first degree programme. Option B states that no direct access is possible, but that access is given to a bridging course. Option C takes the view that access should be granted on the basis of the formal rights in the sending country.

CASE 5	Score	Best	Good	Acceptable	Unacceptable
A No access to a master's programme since the qualification is professionally oriented and does not prepare the individual for research work	7.1	0.0	7.1	42.9	50.0
B No direct access to master's programme, but access to a bridging course preparing for entrance into the master's programme	21.4	14.3	28.6	57.1	0.0
C Access to master's programme, since the qualification gives access to master's programmes in the Netherlands	**64.3**	28.6	50.0	21.4	0.0
D Other	7.1				

The most widespread current practice by far is option C (64%), which also scores highest on best and good practice, and which none of the NARICs found unacceptable. Second comes option B (21% as current practice), which is also found to be acceptable (or better) by all of the NARICs. Option A (no access) scores very low, and is found unacceptable by half the NARICs.

Although this seems a good example of convergent recognition, and leads to a positive recognition decision in most cases, it is remarkable that the formal argument is so strongly favoured. A decision based on learning outcomes is much more likely to result in option B, as it is clearly stated in the description of the case that there are essential elements missing in this bachelor's programme that might make it quite difficult for the student to successfully follow the master's programme. In fact, in the country where the qualification was obtained (the Netherlands) it is very likely that the student will be referred to a bridging course preparing for entrance into the master's programme.

Case 6

CASE 6	
Country of origin	Czech Republic
Qualification	*Vysvedceni o maturitni zkousce* obtained at *Stredni odborna skola* (secondary vocational school)
Purpose of evaluation	Admission to an academic bachelor's programme
Possible substantial difference	The programme is a combination of general and vocational secondary education

In some European countries, admission to university programmes is based on completion of an academically demanding secondary school programme, consisting of general education only, whereas in other European countries combined general and vocational secondary education programmes may also provide admission. This might lead to a substantial difference in the content and learning outcomes of the secondary school programme, which prepares the student for entry onto the academically-oriented bachelor's programme. In this case, a combined general and vocational secondary education programme from the Czech Republic is selected, which exists alongside the more demanding general secondary education programme, leads to the same diploma, and gives access to university programmes in the Czech Republic.

Option A states that admission should be possible, but only to programmes in the same field of study as the vocational part of the programme. Option B denies recognition on the basis of the existing substantial differences, while option C represents the formal point of view that admission should be granted because of the rights in the sending country.

CASE 6	Score	Best	Good	Acceptable	Unacceptable
A Admission to programmes in the same field of study as the vocational part of the secondary education programme	21.4	7.1	14.3	71.4	7.1

CASE 6					
B No admission, because of the substantial differences in contents and learning outcomes	7.1	0.0	0.0	28.6	71.4
C Admission to all bachelor's programmes, since the qualification does give access to higher education in the Czech Republic	**57.1**	35.7	28.6	35.7	0.0
D Other	14.3				

Option C (again the formal one), which was indicated by the majority of NARICs (57%) as their current practice, is also considered best/good practice by the majority and is not found unacceptable by any of them. Option A comes second, with almost a quarter of the votes, and a low score on unacceptability. Option B is very unpopular, and scores a very high 71% for being seen as unacceptable. Remarkably, this option takes into account the substantial differences in learning outcomes of the secondary education programme, so it seems that in this case the formal argument of access in the sending country is considered to be much more important than the actual match of learning outcomes with the entrance requirements of the bachelor's programmes (a result similar to that of Case 5).

Case 7

CASE 7	
Country of origin	Iraq
Qualification	Any degree
Purpose of evaluation	Any purpose
Possible substantial difference	Verification of authenticity is very difficult

This case raises the question of whether the verification of authenticity of diplomas may constitute a substantial difference, since verification is sometimes very difficult in countries with relatively weak infrastructures, and in circumstances where it is hard to establish contacts that could supply reliable information on the authenticity of documents. Such a situation has existed in Iraq, which is why this example was chosen to illustrate the case. How do you evaluate a diploma when you have reason to believe that the chances of it not being authentic are rather high, but it is difficult to verify your suspicions?

There are several ways to go about it. Option A simply states that such diplomas will not be evaluated. Option B states the same, but refers the diploma holders to a national system for evaluation that has been established for refugees who are unable to document their education. Option C takes the stance that all diplomas are evaluated, as it is not the responsibility of the NARIC office to verify authenticity. Option D expresses the view that evaluation is possible on the basis of the expertise in verifying authenticity that has been built up within the NARIC office.

CASE 7	Score	Best	Good	Acceptable	Unacceptable
A Degrees from Iraq are not evaluated because of lack of contacts in Iraq	0.0	0.0	0.0	0.0	100
B Degrees from Iraq are not evaluated, applicants are referred to a system for the evaluation of refugees with no documentation	14.3	7.1	21.4	50.0	21.4
C All degrees from Iraq are evaluated, as authenticity is never verified in our proced-ures	7.1	0.0	7.1	28.6	64.3
D Degrees from Iraq are evaluated, as our office has invested in expertise and methodology to verify their authenticity	**50.0**	64.3	21.4	7.1	7.1
E Other	28.6				

Perhaps not surprisingly, option D has the highest score (50%) in terms of current practice and is also seen by the vast majority as best (64%) or good (21%) practice. These scores clearly indicate that some of the NARICs that did not choose this option are willing to go in this direction but probably lack staff and/or expertise to implement this option. On the other hand, it should be mentioned that the score on unacceptability is not zero (although it is very low), expressing some degree of hesitation on this option. Option B comes in second place (14% as current practice). It also has some support as best/good practice and is rated unacceptable by 21%. This implies that the option of regarding these Iraqi diplomas as "lacking docu-mentation" is viewed as valid by most, as long as an alternative procedure has been established. However, if no alternative procedure exists, the diplomas may not simply be ignored, as 100% of NARICs indicate in both the score and rating of option C. However, the opposite option is also very unpopular: only 7% of respondents do not check authenticity at all, an option which is frowned upon by 64% of respondents, who rate this as unacceptable.

Option E (the alternative option) has a rather high score of 29%, but in effect the procedures described under this extra option may be considered to reflect the descriptions of options B, C and D.

Case 8

CASE 8	
Country of origin	France
Qualification	*Licence* (three-year programme)
Purpose of evaluation	Admission to research-based master's programme
Possible substantial difference	Contents and mode of study (broad range of subjects taken in first two years without much specialisation, predominantly taught course)

Again, this is a case representing a possible substantial difference in an undergraduate programme that may hinder access to the master's programme, not dissimilar to Case 5. This time the contents (broad range of subjects without much specialisation) and mode of study (predominantly taught course) might be the problem. The French example was chosen in view of the fact that the general quality and level of this qualification is usually not doubted, leading to an emphasis on the contents and mode of study.

Option A takes the strict view that access is not possible at all, option B refers the student to a bridging course, while option C states that access should be granted at all times, irrespective of the contents of the programme, since it gives the same formal rights in the home country.

CASE 8	Score	Best	Good	Acceptable	Unacceptable
A No access to master's programme because of the substantial difference in contents (not enough specialisation)	0.0	0.0	0.0	35.7	64.3
B No direct access to master's programme, but access to a bridging course preparing for entrance into the master's programme	28.6	0.0	42.9	57.1	0.0

CASE 8					
C Access to master's programme, irrespective of contents of *licence* programme	**42.9**	21.4	14.3	50.0	14.3
D Other	28.6				

Option C (access to the master's programme) is clearly the most current practice (scoring 43%), followed by option B (29%) and option A (which scores 0%). Option C also receives substantial support as representing best practice (21%), whereas the other two options are not rated as best practice by any of the respondents. However, if we combine the best and good practice scores, it appears that option B scores higher (43%) than option C (36%). Also, the acceptability of option B is undisputed (0% unacceptable practice), while 14% of the respondents think option C is unacceptable. These findings might be interpreted to signify that some NARICs wish to move away from the formal argument to one based on learning outcomes.

Case 9

CASE 9	
Country of origin	Switzerland
Qualification	Bachelor's degree of a hotel school which is not recognised in Switzerland but is accredited by the New England Association of Schools and Colleges (NEASC) in the United States
Purpose of evaluation	Comparability with bachelor's degree of a hotel school in the host country
Possible substantial difference	No accreditation/recognition at national level

Establishing the accreditation status of higher education programmes is not always a straightforward task, as is illustrated in this case, which involves transnational education and differential recognition between a home and host system. Do we always insist on national accreditation/recognition, or is transnational accreditation also acceptable? And what if the programme and degree are Swiss, but the accreditation is American?

In option A, national accreditation/recognition is required, otherwise the degree will not even be evaluated, let alone recognised. Option B indicates that not only is the American accreditation accepted, but the degree is also considered to be comparable to a bachelor's degree. Option C refers to the Revised Code of Good Practice in the Provision of Transnational Education, which is consulted to check whether the degree is awarded in accordance with good practice. Option D accepts the American accreditation, but does not consider this to be sufficient to guarantee the outcome of the programme to be comparable to bachelor's level.

CASE 9	Score	Best	Good	Acceptable	Unacceptable
A Degrees that are not accredited/recognised at national level will not be evaluated	14.3	7.1	7.1	35.7	50.0
B Regional United States accreditation is sufficient (irrespective of location of institution), degree is evaluated as comparable to a bachelor's	28.6	21.4	14.3	50.0	14.3
C The degree is evaluated only after checking that it is awarded in accordance with the Revised Code of Good Practice in the Provision of Transnational Education of 2007	**35.7**	28.6	50.0	21.4	0.0
D Regional United States accreditation is accepted, but does not provide much guarantee of quality and learning outcomes (which will be critically investigated during the evaluation)	21.4	7.1	28.6	50.0	14.3
E Other	0.0				

The results for this case are quite mixed, as all of the four options obtain significant scores. This might indicate that there is some confusion in how to treat such transnational accreditation situations. The winner in terms of current practice is option C (36%), which refers to the Revised Code of Good Practice in the Provision of Transnational Education, but does not give an indication on what the outcome might be in this particular case. Furthermore, it should be noted that this code does not seem to apply, at least in formal terms, to the case described above, as it does not involve transnational education as defined in the code. The most positive option (B) comes second in terms of current practice (29%), followed by option C (21%), while the most negative option (A) scores lowest (14%). Option A is also considered to be unacceptable by 50%, confirming its position as least favoured.

Due to the spread in choice between the four options, we do not consider this to be an example of convergent recognition practice, although there seems to be a clear willingness to take the "foreign" accreditation into consideration.

Case 10

CASE 10	
Country of origin	United States
Qualification	Master's degree (in subject area A that does not represent further specialisation from the previously obtained bachelor's degree in subject area B)
Purpose of evaluation	Admission to doctoral programme in subject area A (similar to that of the master's degree)
Possible substantial difference	Contents (bachelor's programme in subject area B has little relation to master's programme in subject area A)

This case involves a possible substantial difference in contents if a master's programme has been completed in a subject area that does not represent further specialisation from the previously completed bachelor's programme. It also illustrates the potential complications arising from different educational systems having different rules and practices, as regards preparation for graduate studies. In this case, the substantial difference may be seen as lying in the respective profiles of the qualifications. This might be an obstacle for admission to a doctoral programme in the subject area of the master's programme.

Option A considers this difference (the undergraduate part of the programme is lacking in content relevant to the subject area) as too substantial to allow access to the doctoral programme. Option B, on the other hand, would provide access to the doctoral programme on the basis of the learning outcomes of the master's programme.

CASE 10	Score	Best	Good	Acceptable	Unacceptable
A No access to doctoral programme in subject area A, since there is a substantial difference from the contents of the bachelor's programme in subject area B	21.4	7.1	7.1	64.3	21.4

CASE 10	Score	Best	Good	Acceptable	Unacceptable
B Access to doctoral programme in subject area A, on the basis of the learning outcomes of the master's degree in subject area A, irrespective of the contents of the bachelor's programme	**57.1**	28.6	42.9	28.6	0.0
C Other	21.4				

Option B, which clearly represents the most common current practice (57%), is not seen as unacceptable by anyone, and also has the strongest support in terms of being seen as best and good practice. Interestingly, the amount of votes for best/good practice for option B is higher than the percentage of respondents indicating option B as their current practice, whereas the situation is the opposite for option A. Both findings indicate a willingness to move away from option A to option B, and to give more weight to the argument in terms of learning outcomes. On the other hand, a majority of 78% still finds option A acceptable (or better).

Concluding remarks

The main conclusion to be drawn from this survey is that recognition practice in Europe seems rather divided. In some cases, outright controversial issues have been identified – notably in Cases 1, 4 and 9. Yet, even in the more convergent cases, almost all of the options have been scored, and the ratings in terms of good practice for these cases also show that there is lack of general agreement among NARICs on the best way to go.

If we consider the overall outcomes of the 10 cases in terms of recognition, we may distinguish between positive and negative recognition results. Taking into account the scores of all 10 cases, it appears that in only two cases (Cases 1 and 2) the majority of respondents come to a negative evaluation (that is refuse recognition). That in itself may be taken as an indication that European practice in general does not seem to be overly inclined to deny recognition on the basis of possible substantial differences.

The inclusion of several non-European qualifications in the survey did not lead to any comments from NARIC centres that the concept of substantial differences would not be applied to countries that have not ratified the Lisbon Recognition Convention. This seems to indicate that the principles of the convention are widely applied, which indeed is also encouraged by the convention itself. The outcomes of the cases involving non-European qualifications appear to be in line with those of the European qualifications, showing similar trends and tendencies in the options scored and ratings given.

A striking conclusion from this survey is that, in virtually all cases, the formal rights of the qualification in the sending country seem to prevail over any other argument. This may lead to either a more strict or a more lenient outcome, as compared to the evaluations based on learning outcomes. In that sense, there is no clear relationship between reliance on formal, legalistic arguments and the strictness of the outcome. Still, the legalistic approach does not always seem to be favourable from the point of view of the holder of the qualification, as it seems to produce more mismatches between the competencies of the student and the competencies required for entrance into a particular programme. If the student has the right competencies, but is rejected on formal grounds, cross-border mobility is directly hindered. If the student is admitted to a programme, but is lacking in some essential competence(s), the student is not very likely to enjoy a fruitful mobility experience.

Interestingly, the options indicated as the prevailing current practice were not always rated highest in terms of best practice, indicating that NARICs do not always consider their own current practice as the most desirable. This not only indicates that the survey was answered very candidly and in an open-minded spirit, but also hints at the current tendencies in recognition practice. In general, it seems that most NARIC offices are willing to move away from recognition based on legalistic and formal arguments and wish to move towards recognition based on learning outcomes. This seems especially true in cases where formal arguments lead to negative recognition decisions. If the formal argument leads to a positive decision, there seems to be much less willingness to apply criteria in terms of learning outcomes that could lead to a less positive outcome.

Obviously, this outcome is very much in line with the initiatives developed within the Bologna Process. However, it seems that current recognition practice is often governed by national laws and regulations, which have to be followed by NARIC offices. It remains to be seen whether the NARICs' intention to base their recognition practice more firmly on the evaluation of learning outcomes is genuine and whether it will result in major changes in recognition policy. The implementation of the national action plans on recognition would seem to be a good way to judge the actual developments in that direction.

In conclusion, more than 10 years after the adoption of the Lisbon Recognition Convention, there seem to be very few "textbook cases" of substantial differences on which all NARICs agree. A great effort seems to be required in order to narrow down the "bandwidth" of recognition decisions to a more consistent level across Europe. It is hoped that the outcomes of the present survey, which are made available to the ENIC and NARIC networks, may be used as input for future developments in this direction.

Approaches to recognition: a question of two cultures?

Sjur Bergan

The concept of two cultures was originally introduced by C. P. Snow in 1959 and referred to the different approaches of the humanities and natural sciences and the failure of communication between them. While a one-line summary of Snow's theory is certainly too simplistic, and while his thesis is not accepted by all,[32] the concept can, with the necessary caveats, be helpful in describing fundamental differences in people's approach to certain issues. In a different context, I have explored whether the term could meaningfully be used to describe broader differences in approaches to higher education policies.[33] I explored different approaches to the importance of legislation in developing higher education systems and shaping higher education policies, with particular reference to the European Higher Education Area, and I made the point that while laws are absolutely necessary, like medicine, they are effective only if applied in suitable quantities and with room for professional discretion.

The purpose of the present article is to explore two basic differences in attitudes to recognition, and in particular to the concept of substantial differences, which is a key concept of the Council of Europe/UNESCO Recognition Convention, as well as the subject of this book. The two cultural approaches to recognition include a highly legalistic approach and one that, while also based on the provisions of relevant laws, takes a broader view of the circumstances that may lead to recognition or non-recognition. At the risk of oversimplification, one approach may be described as using the law to find reasons not to recognise a qualification – with the reasoning that if recognition is not explicitly permitted, it must be avoided – while the other may be described as using the law to find creative solutions to recognition challenges.

Some caveats are, however, in order. Neither approach can reasonably be described as reflecting an "anything goes" attitude, and neither can be characterised as seeking to obstruct all recognition. Practitioners of both approaches will agree in a good number of cases, either that recognition should be granted or that it should be refused. However, they are likely to disagree on quite a few cases in the grey area between the more clear-cut extremes of the spectrum.

Attitudes to how legislation should be used may be supplemented by another set of differences in approach or culture, namely in credentials evaluators' views of

32. Participants in a Council of Europe project on the heritage of European universities, one of the transnational projects within the "Europe, a Common Heritage" campaign, were divided in their views on whether the concept was relevant to the heritage of their university, cf. Nuria Sanz and Sjur Bergan, *The Heritage of European Universities,* Strasbourg, 2002, Council of Europe Press.
33. Sjur Bergan, "A Tale of Two Cultures in Higher Education Policies: the Rule of Law or an Excess of Legalism?" *Journal of Studies in International Education,* Volume 8, Issue 2, Summer 2004.

what their own roles and priorities should properly be. Is their primary function to protect their own system and qualifications and to make sure that it is not devalued by the recognition of qualifications that may compare unfavourably, or is it to help individual learners by doing everything they can to have their qualifications recognised to the greatest extent possible? Again, at the risk of oversimplification, the former may be thought of as making absolutely sure sure the foreign qualification is precisely equivalent, whereas the latter may be content with less than full recognition and rather looks for broad comparability in level, purpose and standard.

Phrased in these terms, the alternatives may appear Manichean. On the one hand, one has the dour gatekeepers of "the system" and on the other the valiant champions of individual rights and opportunities. As is often the case, reality is somewhat more complex. Recognising substandard qualifications is unfortunate for individuals as well as systems. Arguably, one does individuals no favours by putting them in situations where they cannot cope, and there is a strong risk of doing that if one gives learners access to study programmes for which they are not qualified and for which a hectic catch-up session before the start of the semester, or in the course of the first academic year will not be sufficient. Nor is it helpful, safe or socially responsible to recognise an inferior professional qualification that would permit an inadequately prepared individual to work in a technical or decision-making capacity, and such a mistake may have legal as well as other consequences. Systematically recognising substandard qualifications may also, in the longer run, raise doubts about the higher education system that accepts such qualifications, since this kind of recognition practice could be read as an implicit statement on the quality of one's own system. If one accepts a wide range of less than adequate qualifications, are one's own qualifications adequate? It is important to underline that the debate is not about whether to recognise substandard qualifications, since no serious credentials evaluator would advocate that. Rather, the debate is about what constitutes a comparable qualification and how one goes about setting recognition policy and making recognition decisions.

On the other hand, recognition is undeniably about making things possible. The individual is at the heart of recognition, because it is the individual learner and not the system who submits a qualification and whose future is affected by a recognition decision. Being granted recognition of one's qualifications can open the doors to a better and more satisfying future for the individual concerned, while refusing recognition can close those doors – which in some cases may even mean making it impossible for that individual to stay in the host country. The responsibility of credentials evaluators towards individuals should not be taken lightly, and there is no indication it is. Erring on the side of generosity towards the individual, rather than towards one's own system, instinctively appears to be the decent thing to do. At the same time, however, treating some applicants more leniently could be seen as unfair to others, who fully meet all the requirements. Often, the ideal solution does not exist, and giving the individual applicant the benefit of the doubt may indeed be advisable – provided that the doubt is reasonable.

Identifying substantial differences implies deciding whether a difference between two qualifications is important enough to warrant less than full recognition of the foreign qualification. It is not just a question of identifying reasons that might make it possible to argue that the foreign qualification should be given only partial recognition, or even no recognition at all. It is a question of identifying differences that are so important that refusing full recognition is clearly the better course to take.

No legal text can possibly identify all the possible differences that may be considered "substantial", nor indeed can a book such as this. Identifying substantial differences relies on individual judgment, which is why the question of "two cultures" is important.

As a starting point, the likelihood is that there will be differences between two different qualifications – all the more so if they were delivered by two different institutions in two different countries. Incidentally, in recognition terms it is more meaningful to refer to education systems, rather than to countries, and this is the term I will use henceforth in this article. For students considering whether to undertake all or a part of their education abroad, it would also make little sense to look for a programme exactly equivalent to one they could find at home. To speak in the language of modern management, the "added value" would be close to zero, whereas the added costs might easily be quite high.

It might be useful to keep in mind that – as argued elsewhere in this book – qualifications can be seen to comprise five key elements:

- quality
- workload
- level
- profile
- learning outcomes.

To illustrate different approaches, it may be useful to consider whether and in what situations differences in quality may be considered substantial.

There is broad agreement that quality is essential to recognition. Nobody wants to recognise qualifications that are not of sufficient quality. There is, however, less agreement on how good quality is defined and identified, even though there is broad agreement that a qualification of good quality is one that makes the holder qualified – some would say "well qualified" – to pursue further studies in a given field, or exercise a given occupation. In principle, this is a reasonable enough approach, but if the purpose is defined too narrowly, the approach becomes less meaningful. A second degree in mathematics, from a well considered higher education institution, will normally be of good quality and fit for access to a doctoral programme or for exercising a range of occupations. However, it may not be well suited for giving access to a doctoral programme in history, or for employment as an airline pilot – even if pilots do need a solid understanding of mathematics and modern historians need to understand and use quantitative data. The issue here, however, is not one of quality, but concerns the profile of the qualification.

In the same vein, if the [European] qualification in question were not a second degree but a first degree in mathematics from the same well-respected higher education institution, it would normally not give direct access to a doctoral programme in any discipline, even in mathematics. That, however, does not mean that the institution does not provide first degree qualifications of good quality. It simply means that one should not confuse quality and level. The first degree in question would most likely give access to a second degree programme in mathematics, as well as qualify the holder for various occupations – albeit not at the same level as the occupations open to a holder of a second degree. Again, that does not imply a lack of quality, but rather that the first degree in question is of good quality for the purposes for which it is intended and that one should not expect it to meet purposes for which it was not intended.

Credentials evaluators would also need to be aware that a number of non-European systems do permit first-degree holders to enrol in preliminary studies for the doctorate without necessarily already possessing a second degree. This is not direct entry to the doctorate itself, but rather entry into preliminary graduate studies that may lead to candidacy for the doctorate and may provide the basis for earning a master's degree, or passing special examinations and demonstrating research competence, en route to doctoral student status. Such programmes simply indicate that different higher education systems may have differing routes to the same end and that in some subjects the possession of an intermediate master's degree conveys no professional advantage and may be optional. Careful examination of these systemic differences, however, would also show that they do not permit immediate entry into doctoral research from the first degree, but only after a structured set of preparatory studies and examinations, and thus are different in format but not necessarily in purpose, quality or even level.

If someone actually sought to use qualifications in the academic study of mathematics as the basis for seeking recognition as a pilot or a historian, we would in fact be faced with substantial differences unless there were other evidence of relevant training or academic study, or the applicant intended to obtain the relevant education and was seeking to do so. Changing a subject is not per se a substantial difference, and even seeking to study a different subject at a higher level may be acceptable, so long as the student has studied in a closely-related field, has some background in the field, or is willing to undertake the necessary preparation. University programmes already exist across Europe that encourage or recruit students who have studied in one field to undertake another, and joint degree programmes also exist.[34]

---

34. One only needs to note the students who already enter graduate business or public administration programmes from other subjects; who decide to study the history or philosophy of one of the sciences after a first degree in a science subject; who obtain post first degree teaching qualifications in a subject area; or other examples, to realise that changing subjects and levels is no longer a rare or impossible thing even in the EHEA or elsewhere.

With relation to access to a study programme that would imply "skipping" a level, the issue is more complicated. But, even in cases such as this, it is advisable to understand the structure of programmes in other systems that permit this flexibility, under which circumstances they do so, and the obvious fact that other systems have not necessarily experienced the European transition from the former "long cycle" degrees to the post-Bologna two-cycle structure. The conclusion of a credentials evaluator who denied recognition on the basis of substantial differences might in both cases be defensible. However, the credentials evaluator would be drawing his or her conclusion on the basis of misguided arguments, if the decision were argued in terms of a substantial difference in quality rather than profile in the first case and level in the second, and if no allowance were made for programme structure or legitimate systemic differences.

Suppose, however, that a credentials evaluator were asked to assess a foreign second degree in mathematics for the purpose of access to a third degree (doctoral) programme in mathematics. There is no difference in level or profile, but the credentials evaluator argues that there is a substantial difference in quality between the two institutions and hence the two qualifications. Whether that is a defensible argument or not may depend on a number of factors.

One possibility is that the institution or programme from which the qualification was issued has undergone, but failed, a quality assurance assessment. Alternatively, it has never undergone one, or has no evidence of recognition or approval in its system. If this assessment has been carried out according to well-established criteria, such as the Standards and Guidelines for Quality Assurance in the European Higher Education Area,[35] or the published standards for institutions belonging or according to United States or Canadian accreditation standards, the Australian Qualifications Framework or similar standards, then that would be a strong indication that the qualification is in fact of insufficient quality. Few if any credentials evaluators would argue that in this case, the argument of substantial difference in terms of quality would be valid.

However, an institution might not have undergone a quality assessment either because it has not sought to do so, or because it has not had an opportunity to do so. In this case, can the lack of quality assessment be taken as an indication of lack of quality? Absence of proof is, of course, not the same as proof of absence, and it is difficult to argue that an institution that has not undergone quality assessment is automatically of insufficient quality. However, many credentials evaluators would still consider the lack of quality assessment as a substantial difference, particularly if they operate in a legalistic recognition culture that allows little or no discretion or reference to other evidence of quality besides official recognition.

It is perhaps important to underline that lack of quality assessment is not the same as lack of information about the institution. If credentials evaluators do not know

---

35. www.ond.vlaanderen.be/hogeronderwijs/bologna/documents/Standards-and-Guidelines-for-QA.pdf.

whether an institution has undergone quality assessment, they should seek to find out. In our imagined example, however, the credentials evaluator has managed to establish that the institution has not undergone assessment, and it is then a question of whether it is reasonable for the credentials evaluator to leave it at that and consider the lack of assessment a substantial difference, or alternatively to try to go beyond that and find out more about the quality of the institution.

Here, credentials evaluators may well take different views. One factor is the resources at the credentials evaluator's disposal. While this may be seen as irrelevant from the applicant's point of view, in reality someone who is faced with a high number of applications and has few resources to deal with them is less likely to spend extra time tracking down supplementary information than someone who has a better balance between workload and available resources. It may also depend on why the institution has not undergone assessment. If the institution had ample opportunity to be assessed but did not wish to be, that is unfortunate for the holders of qualifications from that institution, but the onus could legitimately be put on the institution and not on a credentials evaluator. If, on the other hand, the institution had no realistic possibility to undergo quality assessment, either because the public authorities in the country where it is based offer no internationally accepted quality assurance system; because it is barred from undergoing standard quality assurance as its type is excluded (often typical of religious or governmental institutions); or because the institution does not belong to a national education system, credentials evaluators may be more inclined to seek supplementary information.

The attitude may further depend on how likely it is that credentials evaluators will be able to identify reliable supplementary information with reasonable efforts. Institutions from countries with no well-established quality assurance systems, as well as cross-border providers, may in fact have opportunities to undergo quality assessment, and these opportunities are likely to improve over the next few years as quality assurance agencies are less and less bound to operate solely within the territorial jurisdiction in which they are based. The European Quality Assurance Register for Higher Education (EQAR),[36] which was established in 2008, aims to provide an overview of agencies that operate in accordance with the Standards and Guidelines for Quality Assurance in the European Higher Education Area. In principle, assessments carried out by an agency in the EQAR should be accepted by other countries in the European Higher Education Area, regardless of where the agency concerned and the institution being assessed are located. Accrediting agencies in non-European systems, such as the United States and others, have established standards for quality-assuring cross-border institutions and programmes that are accepted by most, if not all, European countries, and many of these may be expected to join the EQAR in the near future.

Credentials evaluators may also have knowledge of the broader situation that might help them judge the qualification, even if precise information on the quality

---

36. www.eqar.eu/index.php?id=32.

assessment or accreditation of a specific institution is lacking. The internationally administered University of the West Indies, or the various UN university and tertiary training establishments are not formally accredited by a national authority, but no reasonable credentials evaluator would argue there is a substantial difference on that basis. On the other hand, some higher education institutions, and even some systems, may have a well-deserved reputation for lack of transparency, or a host institution may have observed over the years that students from a given country or certain institutions tend to be inadequately prepared for further study at the host institution. The point about an institution being assessed according to well-established criteria is also important. Diploma mills – providers that charge fees for delivering diplomas that require no academic work – are now being supplemented by accreditation mills, which deliver bogus accreditation statements, according to a similar scofflaw business model.

Ultimately, however, if in spite of their best efforts and their knowledge of the circumstances of an institution, credentials evaluators cannot establish that the institution is of adequate quality, most of them will probably consider the lack of quality assessment as a substantial difference.

What if an institution has been quality-assessed according to well-established criteria but the credentials evaluator feels – or is obliged to insist – that these criteria do not quite meet the standards of the host country since it is not accredited nationally? And suppose that the criteria for becoming a "national university" are all but impossible for any international institution to meet, due to legal restrictions, and there is no mechanism for recognising the legitimate status of the home country accreditation, even for limited purposes, and even if the institution in question is compliant with all the expectations of guidelines such as the Code of Good Practice in the Provision of Transnational Education? In at least one European country, it seems to be quite common practice for the country to conduct its own assessment of foreign institutions. In its national action plan for recognition, this country outlines the following procedure:

> 1. A review of the foreign higher education institution by a scientific committee of university professors to determine whether it is "essentially equivalent" to that country's higher education institutions.

> 2. An assessment of the particular Department and the program the student attended is made, considering parameters such as admission requirements, number of professors who are PhD holders, teaching and examination procedures and degree titles awarded.[37]

In this case, the host university not only disavows the quality assurance system of the home country of the applicant, but assumes it is itself a competent authority – in both the legal and the substance sense of the term – to quality assess a foreign institution. Here, it is no longer the absence of quality assurance according

37. Quoted from Andrejs Rauhvargers and Agnese Rusakova "Report to the Bologna Follow Up Group on the Analysis of the 2007 National Action Plans for Recognition", Strasbourg/Rīga 2008, internal document, pp. 28-29.

to well-established criteria that is seen as a substantial difference, but the absence of quality assurance by the receiving institution. It is very difficult to see how this could possibly be considered a reasonable interpretation of the concept of substantial difference.

This brief and incomplete consideration of just one of the elements that make up a qualification – quality – serves to illustrate some of the complexity of determining what may reasonably constitute a substantial difference. We examined some situations where it is either clear that there is a substantial difference, or that there is not. In the latter case, we also saw, however, that in at least one country credentials evaluators in effect define as a substantial difference something that would clearly not be considered as such by most evaluators, even if the country in question does not use the term "substantial difference".

Between the two extremes, however, we also saw that there are situations in which credentials evaluators are likely to take different actions. Some of these concern the extra effort credentials evaluators are willing to put into identifying information. It may well be argued that this does not properly speaking constitute a substantial difference, but it does give an indication of factors that may be so considered. It also points to possible differences in attitudes towards applicants: credentials evaluators who see their task as seeking to make recognition possible are likely to put more effort into identifying supplementary information that may help the applicant than are those who see their task primarily as protecting their own system.

The case studies that make up an important part of this book also illustrate different approaches to the concept of substantial differences.

In their overview of the NARIC survey on substantial differences, based on 10 real life cases, Bas Wegewijs and Lucie de Bruin show that while responses to concrete cases varied, between one fifth and one third of the centres that responded to the survey seemed to base their answers more on considerations of a legal nature than on seeking to identify learning outcomes. It may be worth noting that the questionnaire at the basis of the survey provided respondents with clearly formulated alternatives, which would not be the case in real-life situations where credentials evaluators would have to reach a decision – or formulate advice to another competent authority – from scratch. It is difficult to say whether the availability of pre-formulated alternatives may have influenced the responses, either by spelling out alternatives that may have been less obvious to some respondents or by signalling that a set of answers may be acceptable.

It is also difficult to say whether the context of the survey – which could be read to imply that there was a general encouragement to justify decisions in terms of learning outcomes rather than procedures – might have influenced respondents, so that some may have justified their answers in terms of learning outcomes, whereas in their actual practice they would have emphasised formal aspects more strongly. There is little reason to believe that the survey results show too low a percentage of responses emphasising formal arguments, but on the other hand, there is also reason to believe that since most respondents were seasoned professionals, they would answer in accordance with their actual practice.

Actual practice does, of course, not always correspond to desirable practice – even in the eyes of those responsible for the practice. There may, for example, be legal or procedural restraints that oblige credentials evaluators to make decisions based on criteria that are different from those they would ideally have liked to use. Wegewijs and de Bruin's article shows this very clearly. For example, in their first case – recognition of a South African bachelor's degree in history – 53%[38] of the respondents would have made their decision on the basis of criteria and procedures that only 46% of them characterised as best or good practice. Conversely, only some 27% of respondents would have made their decision on the basis of an assessment of learning outcomes, whereas 67% of the respondents felt this alternative represented best or good practice. In another of the cases in this survey – the one involving a Russian *Kandidat Nauk* – 20% of respondents would have used a criterion that none characterised as best practice and only 7% as "good".

The fictitious example described by Erwin Malfroy, that of an applicant holding a Master of Arts in Psychological Sciences, illustrates the interplay in many assessments between formal and content aspects of the qualification. Malfroy's case in particular illustrates that legal regulations on regulated professions may, by themselves, constitute a decisive element in the recognition decision. At the same time, the discussion of this case points to factors such as possible differences between the programmes and institutions from which the qualification was earned, as well as workload, as possible substantial differences. Equally, the article points out that such differences are not necessarily substantial, and that other factors may override differences here. Not least, Malfroy's article illustrates the importance of considering learning outcomes in a discussion of possible substantial differences. Indeed, if the learning outcomes of two qualifications are broadly similar, it would seem difficult to argue that differences in forms or procedure nevertheless constitute substantial differences that would overrule the similarity in learning outcomes.

Both the initial considerations in this article and the case studies included in this volume demonstrate that there are different approaches to recognition, and that the approach which a given credentials evaluator chooses depends on a range of factors that may, taken together, justify reference to differences in culture, without falling into the trap of thinking of the world of credentials evaluation as divided into two stark camps.[39]

Nor is the difference only apparent between different credentials evaluators. Since the responses showed that many credentials evaluators would have preferred

---

38. For the sake of readability, all percentages have been rounded. This does not affect the argument.
39. With reference to societies in which all or most major societal divides coincide, so that people who vote for a given party also overwhelmingly tend to belong to the same socio-economic group, religion, ethnic background, language and so on, for which the Dutch political scientist Arend Lijphart coined the term *verzuiling* (pillarisation).

to decide differently than they have done, on the basis of different criteria and procedures, we must also draw the conclusion that there are, at least in many of the cases referred to in this book, differences in perception between those who decide on the overall legislation, regulations and policy and those who implement recognition policy.

Do the differences amount to a difference between "two cultures" in recognition, as suggested in this article? We have seen that in most cases we are not faced with a clear choice of right or wrong and that there are many shades of grey in the world of credentials evaluation. Nevertheless, there are important differences in attitude between credentials evaluators and between the national rules and policies that different credentials evaluators work with. These are differences between individuals, but to an extent also between countries and cultures. Some individuals, as well as some cultures, seem to be more rule bound than others, whereas other individuals and other cultures seem to be more open to considering a range of factors in their assessment.

Credentials evaluators cannot decide against the legal regulations of the country or system in which they work. However, for countries that have ratified the Council of Europe/UNESCO Recognition Convention, this convention as well as its subsidiary texts should be a key part of the legal basis on which recognition decisions are made.

The current discussions about qualifications[40] include consideration of subject-specific and transversal competences. Subject-specific competences relate to the specific discipline(s) in which a given qualification is obtained, such as history or chemistry, whereas transversal competences designate the knowledge, understanding and ability to do that any higher education graduate at a given level should have, regardless of his or her academic specialisation.[41] Among the transferable competences identified by the Tuning project are:

— the ability to analyse and synthesise;

— the ability to organise and plan;

— the ability to communicate orally and in writing in one's native language as well as in foreign languages;

— problem solving;

— decision making;

— critical and self-critical abilities;

— ability to communicate with experts in other fields;

— ability to work in an international context;

---

40. For a detailed consideration, see Sjur Bergan, *Qualifications. Introduction to a Concept*, Council of Europe Higher Education Series No. 6, Council of Europe Publishing, Strasbourg, 2007.

41. The distinction between subject-specific and transversal competences was explored by the TUNING project, see www.relint.deusto.es/TUNINGProject/documentos/Tuning_phase1/Portada_listapart_mapa_indice%20page1a16.pdf.

- ability to apply knowledge in practice;

- ability to learn;

- ability to generate new ideas (creativity);

- understanding of cultures and customs of other countries;

- initiative and entrepreneurial spirit.

Good credentials evaluators must know the subject-specific aspects of recognition, that is they must, among other things, know and understand the concept of qualifications, their own as well as the international legal framework for recognition and the education systems of foreign countries. They cannot be experts in all education systems, but they must know where they can find information on the systems of countries with which they are not well acquainted, and they must be able to assess that information.

Equally important, however, are the transversal competences that credentials evaluators should have. One cannot identify substantial differences on the basis of subject-specific competences alone. Identifying substantial differences implies an ability to ask critical questions as well as the ability to find a reasonable answer to those questions. The answer to the question "why might the difference between qualification A and qualification B be considered substantial?", or even more importantly, "why *should* the difference between qualification A and qualification B be considered substantial?" may be found in the legal framework, perhaps especially in the case of regulated professions, but more often it requires careful analysis of the purposes for which recognition is sought.

The essential question is "why do the learning outcomes the applicant has obtained make him able or unable to follow a given study programme or exercise a given employment?" Answering that question satisfactorily requires a mix of subject-specific and transversal competences. It requires that the credentials evaluator be able to assess not only a candidate's past achievement but also their future potential. It requires that the recognition decision be made on the basis of knowledge and understanding of the qualification in question and of the role and function of that qualification. It requires knowledge of the legal framework, but the decision should not be made without exercising a quality for which there can be no legal provision: common sense.

Developing the appropriate combination of subject-specific and transversal competences and not least the ability to exercise common sense is one of the main purposes of the ENIC and NARIC networks and of their consideration of the concept of substantial differences. In this author's view, there are still differences in approach that justify the idea of "two cultures" in this area, but it is also this author's hope that through continued consideration of the issue, these differences in approach will diminish. The ultimate goal must be that applicants will have the assurance that wherever they apply for recognition, their applications will be considered with the same professionalism and the same openness of mind with which the credentials evaluators would like their own qualifications to be assessed.

Qualifications from non-recognised institutions: an overview of the issue

E. Stephen Hunt

At the outset, one might fairly ask: "Why is this an issue?", "What sort of non-recognised institution could possibly meet the requirements for recognition under European and Lisbon Recognition Convention guidelines?" The answer to these questions, as it is to others, is that it depends. Let me elaborate.

The documentary framework

The Lisbon Recognition Convention does not address the issue of non-accredited institutions directly. It defines a higher education institution (I.1) as: "An establishment providing higher education and recognised by the competent authority of a Party as belonging to its system of higher education." Notwithstanding the apparent restrictiveness of this definition, the convention and the accompanying explanatory report contain several references that appear to permit, or at least not exclude, a wider institutional focus.

– The definitions of a qualification and recognition give the national authorities the final say as to what constitutes a recognisable educational outcome.

– The convention expressly permits members to use recognition standards that are more favourable than those discussed in the convention (II.3).

– The "Basic principles" (Section III) are not explicitly restricted to cases where a recognition request involves a recognised institution.

– While the section on the "Recognition of higher education qualifications" is not explicitly restrictive (IV), it does permit members to impose requirements via their national laws and policies (IV.5).

– The section on "Refugee qualifications" (VII) is totally unrestricted.

– The section on "higher education programmes and institutions" (VIII.1) simply asks the recognising party to ascertain the status of the institution, and recognises that some institutions may not belong to a formally assessed system (VIII.1b).[42]

While the Lisbon Recognition Convention clearly assumes that most qualifications, institutions and programmes will be recognised, it does not limit what can be

---

42. The latter provision should, however, be seen in its proper context. In 1997, when the convention was adopted, there was still discussion about whether a formal system of quality assurance was needed. Today, there is broad consensus that formal quality assurance is required, and it is difficult to imagine that a party to the convention could fulfil its obligation under this section without reference to its quality assurance system.

recognised and it does not exclude the possibility that some non-recognised institutions might be included under some circumstances.

The explanatory report alludes to the increasingly complex diversity of institutional types (pp. 3-4, paragraphs 4 and 5) and the evolution away from the old model of clearly delineated educational systems. The statement on recognition practice (p. 5, paragraph 13) also points towards flexibility as the new model. And the discussion of institutional and programmatic assessment contains the noteworthy statement that: "The Convention should not be read as taking a stand on particular mechanisms or methods of quality assurance, nor on the relative importance of institutional assessment and quality assurance" (p. 9). It is even noted on page 11 that "…institutions which are not considered as belonging to the higher education system of a Party may offer some higher education programmes", including those offering programmes to students not their own. However, parties may consider education acquired at an institution not belonging to the higher education system of the home country as constituting a substantial difference (p. 23).

The evidence available from the Lisbon Recognition Convention and its explanatory report points to a clear preference that institutions and programmes be recognised by some appropriate mechanism in the home country. It is not mandatory that this should be so, but it is desirable. And it is clear that ENICs and NARICs, as well as other competent authorities, may treat non-recognised institutions under the substantial difference provision if they so choose. Such a provision would adequately cover cases of institutions that have been denied accreditation or recognition, or have not sought it, for the traditional reasons: substandard quality or capacity, or fraud (bogus institutions).

If the institution is not recognised because it cannot achieve accreditation or some similar type of recognition, either because it is substandard or because it is bogus, then clearly the onus falls upon the institution, not the recognition authority. It may be possible to exercise some limited discretion in cases where the institution is real but inadequate, depending on what the inadequacy is and the circumstances of the individual case. But it is not possible, or even desirable, to waive normal recognition requirements for a bogus institution that, by its nature, has no intention of providing serious education.

Transnational or cross-border institutions

The problem of non-recognised institutions first emerged with the recent rapid increase in institutions providing educational services outside their home system. Cross-border provision of higher education has – contrary to popular belief – actually been around for a very long time. Perhaps the oldest cross-border correspondence institution in the world is the Majlis Al-Ahzar, or Al-Ahzar University, which has provided correspondence syllabi for the instruction of Sunni legal scholars across the Islamic world since at least the 15th century. The external division of the University of London provided correspondence – later a part of the broader concept of distance – degree programmes from the 19th century, and the establishment of overseas US higher education institutions (not branches) started at the end of the 19th century.

Historical examples of transnational higher education were noteworthy for their rarity as well as for either being correspondence (distance) programmes operated within imperial contexts or free-standing institutions serving expatriates of the home country and a few interested students in the host country or region. Following the Second World War, however, the situation began to change. The first significant development was the concept of study abroad, initiated by the United States but since taken up by other countries. Conceptually, study abroad is a modern cousin of the medieval *Wanderjahr,* except that the modern version began as a study opportunity arranged, taught and credited by the home institution and has only recently evolved into genuine inter-system academic mobility under the auspices of Erasmus Mundus and related programmes. The concepts of branch campuses and franchise programmes followed the advent of study abroad programmes. Branch campuses arose because some study abroad programmes became so successful, and so large, that it was more practical to simply set up an overseas branch of the parent institution rather than continue to administer the programme remotely from home. Many successful study abroad programmes had evolved partnerships with host country institutions and faculties, but were not intended to be or capable of becoming branch campuses. Thus the concept of the franchise programme arose whereby a host institution – often, but not always, a recognised institution – would provide the infrastructure and much of the faculty for programmes organised and overseen by the overseas partner.

While these forms of transnational higher education began in many cases as US initiatives, especially during the decades of the 1960s through the 1980s, study abroad programmes, branch campuses and franchises are now operated by many institutions representing a wide variety of countries, including Europe. And they have become a global phenomenon, not just a transatlantic one. The recognition of qualifications earned at these institutions has also evolved from early resistance (including inside the United States) to gradual acceptance of such providers, so long as they possess institutional recognition in the home system (at least), and recognition in the host system if they purport to offer national qualifications recognised in that system. More typically, they are simply treated as foreign institutions freely operating in a host country and their qualifications are treated as degrees from their home system. The ENIC and NARIC networks developed and implemented the Code of Good Practice in the Provision of Transnational Higher Education, revised in 2007, to address the recognition of legitimate transnational institutions and their credits and qualifications. This code in turn became an important document in the drafting of the UNESCO-OECD Guidelines for Quality Provision in Cross-Border Higher Education, adopted in 2007.

What emerged next, however, is the phenomenon that has created a continuing set of difficulties for recognition authorities: the Internet and electronic distance education. The World Wide Web was publicly launched in 1993, just prior to the formation of the ENIC Network and the negotiation of the Lisbon Recognition Convention. It has grown exponentially ever since. And three parallel developments in higher education have grown alongside it: (1) the development of web presences and online programmes, many interactive, by most established traditional institutions as a means to attract new students; (2) the advent of specialised distance institutions, both state supported and private; and (3) the development of online bogus institutions and other frauds, masquerading as legitimate providers.

It must be noted that distance education per se is not the problem. Distance education and its pre-electronic predecessor, correspondence education, have been around for hundreds of years. Many nations, including most of those in the European Higher Education Area (EHEA), North America and the Asia-Pacific Economic Co-operation (APEC), have officially recognised distance institutions offering recognised degree programmes as well as short courses. While there have been difficulties in evolving adequate quality assurance mechanisms for this type of education, most of those problems have been overcome and today nationally recognised quality assurance agencies are generally able to evaluate distance programmes just as they do traditional programmes. The difficulty is not in identifying and recognising legitimate distance education offered by accredited institutions. Rather, it is in identifying and dealing with the proliferation of bogus providers, and a growing network of bogus accrediting bodies, which mimic genuine providers, post inaccurate and misleading information that is difficult to check, have no legitimate home system – or move around several systems, and exploit the freedom of the Internet to hide their ownership and victimise both consumers and responsible authorities.

This overview will address the matter of substandard and bogus institutions in a few paragraphs. First, however, it is necessary to deal with a much smaller but nonetheless serious aspect of non-recognised higher education. This is the presence of legitimate institutions which are non-recognised, due to factors other than academic quality, administrative competence or fraud.

Legitimate non-recognised institutions

What if an institution is demonstrably legitimate but is non-recognised because its problem lies with the recognition process itself? Suppose that an institution can be shown to meet the qualitative and administrative requirements for recognition, in either the home or the host system or both, and is in fact acknowledged by the authorities in its system, yet the prevailing regulations or policies cannot deal with it because it is the wrong type of institution, or is operated by a non-education agency, or is operated by the "wrong" faith community or organisation, or is simply privately controlled rather than state-funded? Even if its students are admitted to courses in recognised institutions and the institution has relationships with these institutions? Are these factors to be considered insuperable barriers to recognition, or even a "substantial difference"?

The problem here is that strict adherence to narrowly focused requirements may occasionally exclude legitimate institutions, and legitimate graduates, from receiving the fair and transparent assessment required by the Lisbon Recognition Convention. Worse, exclusion from recognition because of religion or association may well violate European laws and agreements on human rights, not to mention the laws of a country that simultaneously guarantees such freedoms yet restricts "non-established" faith communities from getting their institutions approved. And excluding public institutions from recognition simply because they do not fall under the ministry of education's oversight may cause graduates of such institutions – including public officials – to be discriminated against by the government they serve.

There are several distinct types of institutions that may present recognition difficulties even though they can be shown to meet the expectations of the aforementioned code of good practice and guidelines; are in some cases approved and recognised by competent authorities; have formal agreements for articulation and transfer with recognised institutions; and whose graduates not only receive good educations, but are permitted to work alongside individuals with formally recognised qualifications. These are:

–   government institutions, such as military and civil service academies, where the educational programmes are acknowledged to provide instruction at a higher education level, but which are considered outside the formal higher education system for administrative rather than qualitative reasons;

–   institutions that provide direct access to certain types of higher education, or provide higher level instruction in some programmes, but are post-secondary vocational and technical programmes, adult education programmes or programmes in fields such as the arts (or non-higher education government academies), and are not classified as part of the higher education system and whose graduates often face uncertainties;

–   theological seminaries and related religious institutions that provide instruction at a clear higher education level, and which may have arrangements with theological departments at recognised institutions, but which are not recognised because they do not belong to a state-supported or recognised religious faith, rather than due to any academic or administrative deficiency;

–   legitimate transnational institutions that have appropriate recognition in their home system (and the host system if offering national programmes), are permitted to operate by the host country, but do not possess recognition in the host system for reasons of jurisdiction and/or academic curriculum or private status, rather than because of any inability to meet recognition requirements.

The number of institutions falling into the above categories is much smaller than the number of bogus providers. But the difference between these types of institutions and the substandard or bogus variety is profound. One or more of these legitimate types exists in nearly every country. Any approach to the issue of non-recognised institutions needs to be able to distinguish institutions that have some claim to fair treatment by recognition authorities from those that do not.

Categorising non-recognised institutions

The foregoing analysis suggests that there are five broad categories of tertiary education provider that can – for one reason or another – be non-recognised. Each constitutes a different set of circumstances and suggests a different solution.

Category I – Equivalent institutions barred from recognition, or choosing not to be recognised

In many countries, perfectly legitimate institutions may not fall under the jurisdiction of the ministry of education or other competent authority, or may lie outside the legal class of institutions for which public recognition is possible. For example, many government and military educational institutions whose programmes are comparable in content and level to civilian institutions may fall outside the jurisdiction of national quality assurance and recognition authorities. There may be no question as to the quality of these programmes, notwithstanding the fact that they fall outside "normal" channels of recognition. Graduates of these institutions and programmes may be handicapped if they attempt to use their qualifications to enter civilian higher education institutions, or if they attempt to gain authorisation to practise a profession. The consequence is a clash between process and fairness.

Another such example has to do with dedicated religious institutions, such as seminaries. There are many countries where freedom of religion is guaranteed, but which also retain national recognition status for certain faiths. The theological departments and seminaries of these established and state-supported faiths are publicly funded, linked to recognised universities and present no bureaucratic obstacle to recognition. At the same time, there are a number of theological institutions providing education for vocations in non-established faiths, many of which have agreements with established theological faculties, which do not possess state recognition and whose graduates – who have often studied alongside colleagues at public universities – meet obstacles in getting their qualifications recognised, notwithstanding laws guaranteeing freedom of religious expression.

Yet another frequent example of what we may call Category I non-recognised institutions are legitimate transnational institutions, whose behaviour and home country recognition status meet the spirit and letter of the ENIC guidelines, yet which cannot achieve recognition, or choose not to apply for it, because host country laws and administrative practices and policies effectively make this impossible. The qualifications earned by the graduates of these institutions are treated as foreign qualifications, and their holders are usually granted recognition. Indeed, everyone involved in such cases may agree that there is no quality assurance issue. Nevertheless, host country authorities cannot or will not work with these institutions with respect to recognition in the host country. In other cases, the host country may be more or less prepared to co-operate, but the institution does not seek appropriate recognition, either because it does not understand the process or its importance, or because it wishes to offer programmes and qualifications reflective of its home system only and does not consider itself a part of the host country's educational system.

Category I cases are sometimes difficult, but they are always legitimate. Recognition authorities confronted with such situations are not dealing with degree mills, frauds or even substandard qualifications. They are dealing with institutions and qualifications that actually fall "between the cracks" within and between national education systems. It is important, in this author's view, that Category I cases are treated with fairness and that recognition authorities find ways to distinguish them from less worthy examples.

Category II – Non-equivalent institutions and programmes falling outside standard higher education

Nearly every country has within its education system examples of programmes and providers that are not considered to be higher education but which are articulated with higher education in some way, such that graduates are qualified to enter tracks that may lead to higher education access or may permit direct access in some circumstances. The providers of such education are often not recognised institutions in the normal sense, or are not recognised at tertiary level. (An example could be government or military institutions that – unlike Category I – are not in fact tertiary institutions or do not award degrees.) It is also frequently the case – especially in decentralised or federal systems – that these providers are approved at some level beneath the national level, but nevertheless possess some status in the education system.

Within national systems, it is possible to understand the qualifications from these providers and accommodate them in the local education system. Thus, for example, UK and many Commonwealth authorities know how to deal with qualifications based on examinations such as City and Guilds, Cambridge, the various professional bodies, and so forth. German authorities understand the various qualifications and rights of graduates of *Berufsschulen, Fachoberschulen, Fachschulen,* and *Berufsakademien* who hold different secondary qualifications. US authorities understand how to deal with various state-approved programmes as well as post-secondary vocational institutions falling outside recognised accreditation. And so on. A problem arises, however, when these post-secondary, non-higher education, and highly country-specific programmes and qualifications are presented for recognition in other systems. While a good deal of progress is being made within the European Union's Europass Network, there remain quite a number of points of difference that need to be addressed, especially if the goal is to evolve a clearly articulated framework by which citizens can progress from secondary, through vocational, to higher studies.

Category II cases can also be confusing and difficult, particularly if inadequate information exists for understanding exactly what a qualification represents and what its prerequisites were. It is also usually clear that – unlike Category I cases – full recognition of such qualifications as equivalent to a higher education degree is unlikely. Nevertheless, Category II cases are also legitimate and do represent some type and level of educational attainment. In many instances it may be possible to fit the qualification holder into some point in the education system. The challenge is to ascertain whether the provider and the qualification have adequate quality and how to analyse the situation for comparability.

Category III – Pre-Bologna and other historical providers and qualifications

This is a special category, in part peculiar to the EHEA, but that affects anyone – European or non-European – who graduated from an institution or programme that either no longer exists, or exists today in a different form or with a different status than before.

Most countries possess records and policies that permit graduates of defunct institutions and programmes to obtain recognition for their past work, so long as the institution or programme in question was properly accredited and recognised at the time the student graduated. Problems may arise, however, if such records have not been kept, have been discarded, or if the current competent recognition authority has no access to them or has difficulty verifying the documents presented by a recognition applicant. Likewise, in many systems there have been profound changes, in which previously existing institutions have been renamed or merged and undergone other modifications to their programmes and qualifications. Are these to be considered new institutions or changed institutions? And what about the qualifications issued prior to the reforms?

Another category of historical problem, and one especially relevant to the EHEA, is what to do with qualifications that signified one thing in the "pre-Bologna" era and another since, even though the qualification itself, the issuing institution and the actual learning outcomes have not changed. At the same time that the Bologna reforms were occurring, many European countries revised their education systems in ways that modified previous tertiary vocational/non-university/university classifications. A qualification from a UK university that was formerly a polytechnic or a further education college, or from a German *Fachhochschule* that once was considered non-university in level but now awards university degrees for the same work, are but two examples of this phenomenon. National competent recognition authorities need to possess fair and transparent policies for what to do in such cases and the ability to communicate these to third countries. Is the nurse who graduated 20 years ago with what was then called a vocational diploma less qualified than her daughter, who graduated in nursing from the same institution and the same programme last year, when both are licensed nurses and both have the same competences, if the institution has been reclassified as a university during those 20 years?

If there is a substantial difference in such cases, how is it to be determined? Under the Lisbon Recognition Convention, the determination of a substantial difference should not simply be based on the reclassification, but rather on genuine differences in learning outcomes, if any, and the purpose for which recognition is sought. And for defunct or merged institutions, is it fair to put the entire burden of documentation on the graduate who had no idea that his or her alma mater would close or be folded into a new entity, or that a recognition decision would be needed decades later, due to a job or relocation change? What policies can be developed that are reasonable and fair to all concerned?

Category IV – Substandard tertiary education providers

Many tertiary providers exist that do not fit into Category I, II or III, yet do not qualify as outright frauds. These are institutions that have tried and failed to attain accreditation or recognition, have been dropped from recognition yet still exist, or have never attempted recognition and most likely would fail if they tried. The qualifications and credits earned at such institutions are unlikely to be accepted by accredited institutions or knowledgeable employers. In most such cases, recognition is either impossible or can be granted only if evidence is presented to show that a particular case is exceptional.

In some cases, such as in the United States, so-called "rules of thumb" have been developed to deal with the odd occurrence of a graduate of a Category IV institution attempting to enrol in an accredited programme or apply for a job. One method is to research the history of graduates of the institution in question. If the institution has a track record of graduates enrolling in high-quality programmes and succeeding, notwithstanding its general problems, then institutions and employers may choose to exercise discretion. A similar situation exists when a person is discovered to have a degree from a Category IV institution, but also has a subsequent degree, legitimately earned from an accredited institution. An employer or institution may exercise discretion in such cases as well, taking note of the fact that the individual has shown that she or he can succeed in legitimate studies, notwithstanding a past mistake. It should be noted, however, that such mercy is the exception, not the rule, and that accrediting agencies generally frown upon legitimately accredited institutions enrolling graduates of unaccredited institutions. And while practice may vary among private employers, public sector employers generally have no flexibility if the job requirement states that graduation from an accredited or recognised programme is mandatory.

Substandard unaccredited institutions can usually be identified, albeit indirectly. In addition to not appearing on any lists of accredited or recognised institutions, they will usually appear in lists of unaccredited institutions whose degrees are not accepted. Category IV institutions can be distinguished from outright frauds because the term "diploma mill" or "degree mill" will not be used, and the legitimacy of the entity will usually be acknowledged. They can also be identified from the lists of institutions dropped from accreditation rolls, but which do not show up in any subsequent accreditation lists.

Category IV cases have to be treated with caution. In principle, neither the institution nor the qualification meets the usual recognition requirements. The question – if there is one – is whether the recognition authority has any discretion and whether there are any mitigating circumstances indicating that the individual applying for recognition has a concrete accomplishment, such as a subsequent qualification or licence, that is legitimate and could be accepted as evidence that they are deserving of some recognition.

Category V – Degree/diploma mills and related frauds

The last category is also by far the largest. It is the burgeoning collection of domestic and international operations purporting to mimic legitimate institutions, but that in fact sell qualifications, possess no standards and often no location, frequently claim "accreditation" by equally bogus accrediting bodies or falsely claim recognition from a legitimate source, and exist solely to prey upon unwary consumers.

It can be stated with confidence that no Category V case deserves any recognition at all, although the victim may benefit from some sound counselling on how to select a genuine educational experience.

Many pleas have been made over the years for lists or directories of degree mills. While there are a few unofficial lists, the development of an international official list is very unlikely for good reasons. Erwin Malfroy of the ENIC/NARIC of the Flemish Community of Belgium has summed up some of the obstacles:

–   It is impossible to publish a complete list of all the diploma mills and/or bogus universities. Some are "officially" located in remote microstates, such as small islands, and even the ones located in one's own country will be hard to find, having only a small mailbox. And many of these diploma mills and/or bogus universities rise up, disappear, pop up again with a totally different name, and so on.

–   Diploma mills and/or bogus universities which are not on the list of diploma mills and/or bogus universities, will use this list as a pro forma tool to show that they are not on the list of diploma mills and/or bogus universities and therefore are recognised/accredited ones and will shout (while waving the print-out): "Look our institution is a recognised/accredited one, because it is not on this black list!"

–   If a private (not public) institution, who is entitled to offer recognised/accredited higher education programmes, is accidentally mentioned on the list of diploma mills and/or bogus universities, this will be a catastrophe for that genuine institution and make it very tough for them to prove that they are indeed entitled to offer recognised/accredited higher education programmes.

–   Some diploma mills and/or bogus universities use a similar name to that of a real institution (or even the same name), and if the names of these diploma mills and/or bogus universities are published, there will be serious confusion and the legitimate institutions will suffer.

The author would add another four to this list:

– Most national authorities, and their legal systems, do not have the ability to precisely identify diploma mills or other academic frauds and prosecute. Some countries, such as the United Kingdom, have the authority to protect national diploma titles. And others, such as the United States, have local jurisdictions (Oregon, Michigan, Texas, for example) which have the power to name frauds and prosecute, but only within that local jurisdiction. The US federal government can now deny employment to, or remove from office, any person holding a job earned via an unaccredited qualification.

– It is shameful, but a fact nonetheless, that civil servants, employees and contractors who perform recognition work are often not legally protected if they are sued by an institution, even a diploma mill, or are put under pressure by politically powerful people to grant recognition in a dubious case and refuse to do so. The law must not only provide a transparent way to distinguish fraud from genuine; it must also insulate responsible authorities from civil liability if and when they have to stand their ground.

– International organisations are legally dependent on the nation states who are their members, and their powers cannot supersede that of national authorities unless each member expressly consents. In addition, if they have a sovereign member who is itself supporting diploma mills, as is happening in some countries, then the international organisation is effectively at the mercy of state-supported fraud.

– The time and expense required to identify frauds, list them and update such lists is massive and simply beyond available budgets. Such an undertaking would require more resources than are currently devoted to legitimate recognition work.

There is good news, despite these obstacles. Reliable resources do exist, including some directories, that are accessible and provide assistance in the identification of educational frauds. Some of these include:

Higher Ed Consulting Australia (www.higheredconsulting.com.au/links.html) provides comprehensive updates on legitimate and fraudulent activity in Australia, as well as links to fraud alerts in many other countries.

The website of Oregon Office of Degree Authorization Unaccredited Colleges (www.osac.state.or.us/oda/unaccredited.aspx) provides a comprehensive overview of the issue and annotated discussions of each identified provider, plus links to other US states.

These sites are maintained by Dr George Brown and Mr Alan Contreras, respectively, who are internationally known experts in the area of institutional and accreditation fraud.

Several ENICs, including USNEI – the US Network for Education Information, provide diploma mill and fraud information on their websites, and both UNESCO and the Council of Europe have disclaimers on their education websites stating categorically that they do not accredit or approve institutions, despite fraudulent claims to the contrary.

In addition, experts inside and outside the ENIC Network have joined a listserv on Yahoo! called Global Accreditation Update. It is managed by George Brown and can be subscribed to at Yahoo Groups. The listserv has been very successful in alerting members to new bogus operations, as well as to links among fraudulent operators.

A new tool that has been launched is the UNESCO higher education portal (http://portal.unesco.org/education). This is a homepage with a searchable database that links users directly to national information centres and quality assurance authorities. A direct outgrowth of the UNESCO-OECD guidelines activity, the project supporting the portal has already assisted several less-developed countries in developing national quality assurance information and putting it online.

Conclusion

This exercise has been a brief effort to cover the range of non-recognised institutions which are frequently encountered and for which recognition solutions need to be offered. It has tried to approach each situation mindful of the Lisbon Recognition Convention principle that one should err on the side of positive recognition if possible, even if that recognition can only be partial. In some cases, of course, positive recognition decisions – even partial ones – cannot be and should not be offered. But, in other cases, the situation may call for a positive solution, even if the general policy is not to deal with non-recognised institutions. To do otherwise would be to violate the spirit of the convention as well as other rights of citizens.

Judgment is always a subjective thing, even if ringed by regulations and procedures. In approaching complex and often fuzzy situations such as non-recognised institutions, it is sometimes a good idea to weigh the spirit of recognition against the letter of bureaucratic process. This can work two ways: to identify bogus providers one often has to think outside the box; and to be fair to legitimate institutions that fall "between the cracks" requires similar judiciousness. It is perhaps helpful to end by heeding the wisdom of Seneca:

> Da operam ne quid umquam invitus facias: quidquid necesse futurum est repugnanti, id volenti necessitas non est. Ita dico: qui imperia libens excipit partem acerbissimam servitutis effugit, facere quod nolit; non qui iussus aliquid facit miser est, sed qui invitus facit. Itaque sic animum componamus ut quidquid res exiget, id velimus...
> (*Epistulae morales ad Lucilium, Epistula LXI*)

> [See to it that you never do anything unwillingly: that which is bound to be a necessity if you rebel, is not a necessity if you desire it. This is what I mean: he who takes his

orders gladly, escapes the bitterest part of slavery – doing what one does not want to do. The man who does something under orders is not unhappy; he is unhappy who does something against his will. Let us therefore so set our minds in order that we may desire whatever is demanded of us by circumstances...]

Qualifications frameworks: an instrument to resolve substantial differences?

Sjur Bergan

Introduction

Qualifications frameworks have become a key element of the European Higher Education Area (EHEA),[43] where ministers adopted an overarching framework of qualifications of the EHEA (QF-EHEA) in 2005 and committed to developing national frameworks compatible with the QF-EHEA. The deadline for developing national frameworks was originally set for 2010, but was extended by ministers at their 2009 meeting so that all 46 countries of the EHEA are now committed to developing their national frameworks and preparing them for self-certification by 2012.

While higher education is more internationalised and has come further in the development of qualifications frameworks than other parts of the education system, the concept of qualifications frameworks is by no means limited to higher education. Several of the pioneers in this area developed comprehensive frameworks, covering all parts of their education system. As one example, the Scottish framework – which is distinct from the framework for England, Wales and Northern Ireland – encompasses 12 levels ranging from educational achievements by learners with severe learning disabilities to doctoral qualifications. The European Qualifications Framework for lifelong learning (EQF-LLL)[44] was developed by the European Commission and formally adopted in 2008. It encompasses eight levels from primary school to doctoral qualifications and the 32 countries[45] to which it applies will reference their own qualifications against the EQF-LLL.

Even if qualifications frameworks now play a key role in European higher education and education policies, they are not a European invention. Australia, New Zealand and South Africa were pioneers in developing qualifications frameworks, for somewhat different reasons. In the case of Australia and New Zealand, the main motivations were to make their qualifications more transparent and hence to make them more attractive. In the case of Australia in particular, this was linked to the fact that this country hosts a large number of foreign students who need recognition of their

---

43. See the Bologna web page on qualifications frameworks at www.ond.vlaanderen.be/hogeronderwijs/bologna/qf/qf.asp.
44. Often also referred to simply as EQF. However, EQF-LLL is preferred here in order to emphasise the lifelong learning aspect of this framework and to avoid possible confusion with the QF-EHEA. See http://ec.europa.eu/education/lifelong-learning-policy/doc44_en.htm.
45. All members of the European Union and the European Economic Area, as well as some other countries that participate in relevant EU programmes.

qualifications when they return home or move on to third countries. In the case of South Africa, the main motivation was one of social cohesion. The apartheid era left many South Africans with qualifications that could not be documented and/or had been earned through non-traditional learning paths. A national qualifications framework afforded better opportunities for recognition of qualifications like these. Both of the primary reasons that led to the development of the three pioneering frameworks – improved transparency and greater social cohesion through education – are relevant to the discussion of qualifications frameworks as possible instruments to resolve substantial differences and improve fair recognition of qualifications.

Before moving on to a more detailed consideration of qualifications frameworks, however, the author would like to recognise that Ireland and the United Kingdom – with, as we have seen, separate frameworks for Scotland on the one hand and England, Wales and Northern Ireland on the other – were pioneers in developing national qualifications frameworks in Europe and that Denmark played a crucial role in putting qualifications frameworks on the European higher education agenda through two important Bologna conferences in 2003[46] and 2005[47] as well as through Mogens Berg's chairmanship of the Bologna working group on qualifications frameworks from 2003 until 2007.

Additionally, it is important to emphasise that the development and implementation of a qualifications framework is a prerogative of the national education system. Within the EHEA, decisions have been taken by the co-operating countries to develop and self-certify qualifications frameworks and to tie these to overarching regional frameworks. This has been a voluntary process specific to the EHEA. Even if many countries around the world are in the process of developing qualifications frameworks, or are discussing whether to do so, countries outside Europe often use quite different approaches to qualifications frameworks, or have no national frame-work in a formal sense. What follows pertains primarily to the European context. In no way should it be implied that having a national qualifications framework is expected or required, that it should follow the European model, or that not having a qualifications framework is a substantial difference for non-European countries with respect to European recognition of their qualifications.

The concept of qualifications frameworks

Qualifications may be seen as consisting of five major components (Bergan 2007; see also the same author's conceptual chapter in this volume):

- quality
- workload

---

46. www.bologna-bergen2005.no/EN/Bol_sem/Old/030327-28Copenhagen/030327-28Report_General_ Rapporteur.pdf.
47. www.bologna-bergen2005.no/EN/Bol_sem/Seminars/050113-14Copenhagen/050113-14_General_ report.pdf

- level

- profile

- learning outcomes.

Qualifications specify or certify educational achievements. In the former sense, they describe typical degrees, such as a bachelor's, master's or doctoral degree. In the latter sense, they describe the achievement of a specific learner. In both cases, qualifications describe something specific: a given typical achievement or a given achievement of a given learner. Qualifications frameworks, on the other hand, are more general or systemic. They describe a set of qualifications – a system – and how they fit together. Qualifications relate to individual awards, while qualifications frameworks relate to education systems.

The concept of qualifications frameworks is at the same time both old and new. At one level, it can be argued that any country that has an education system – and that includes all countries of the world except, perhaps, a very few countries where public authority has broken down due to internal strife – has a qualifications framework. In this sense of the term, a qualifications framework is the same as a degree system, and any formalised system of education has a number of degrees at different levels, some – even most – of which can only be obtained if a learner has first obtained one or more degrees at lower levels in the education system.

That, however, is not the sense in which the term is most commonly used. In this second sense – referred to earlier as a "new style qualifications framework" – the term refers not just to the individual qualifications that make up the framework, but in particular to how these qualifications interlink and how learners can move between the different qualifications that make up the framework. This is most often thought of as moving to a higher qualification on the basis of a lower one, and that is perhaps the most common form of movement within a system. However, movement can also be sideways and even downwards. To take only two examples from higher education, someone with a legal qualification, which would normally be at second degree level, may wish to take a second (master's) level degree in economics or a first (bachelor's) degree in public administration.

Qualifications frameworks should also emphasise learning outcomes, and they should describe the generic learning outcomes one can expect learners to obtain for a certain qualification. Learning outcomes describe what learners should know, understand and be able to do on the basis of a given qualification. All three elements are important. Knowledge is of course important but the very traditional view of education that emphasises facts alone – often in the form of rote learning – as the purpose of learning is no longer tenable. Knowledge without understanding can even be dangerous, and higher education is sometimes accused of providing learners with knowledge, but not with the ability to apply that knowledge. This may not be a fair accusation, and those who make it sometimes have a view of higher education that reduces it to an advanced form of preparation for the labour market, but it does emphasise that knowledge must be understood and put to use.

Think of how we learn a foreign language. We must know vocabulary and grammar as well as the rules of pronunciation and usage, but we must also understand them in order to be able to express ourselves in our newly acquired language – to put the language to use. Knowing the different declensions of Russian nouns, adjectives and verbs is a formidable challenge for those who learn Russian as a foreign language, particularly if Russian is their first Slavic language, but understanding how the rules work in practice is a requirement for being able to speak and write Russian, which is the likely goal of most of those who take up the language.

While describing what a learner knows, understands and is able to do is the traditional definition of learning outcomes, this author has increasingly come to believe that a description of a learner's attitudes should be added to the definition. This is rooted in the view that higher education serves a variety of purposes. In addition to preparing learners for the labour market – the purpose that is most prominent in public debate, at least in Europe – higher education should also prepare learners for life as active citizens in democratic societies, an area in which many US higher education institutions have better enunciated policies than do their European counterparts (Association of American Colleges and Universities, 2007). Higher education should contribute to learners' personal development and it should provide society with a broad and advanced knowledge base (Council of Europe, 2007; Bergan, 2005). Developing attitudes of societal engagement and commitment to democracy and intercultural dialogue are, in this author's view, essential generic learning outcomes for higher education.

Qualifications frameworks thus combine a description of learning paths – the different ways in which learners may move within the system and earn qualifications – and learning outcomes. Formal aspects are not absent from the description of qualifications frameworks, but they play a less prominent role than in the description of traditional education or degree systems. The intention is that the emphasis shift from institutions to learners, from provision to learning, and from formal procedures to content.

Qualifications frameworks, then, describe qualifications in terms of level and learning outcomes. They will often give an indication of the workload typically required to reach the qualification, but they will recognise that this is an indication only and that there are several learning paths to the same qualification. Workload will also depend on previous learning outcomes: a learner who is already proficient in a Slavic language will obtain a given level in Russian more rapidly than a learner for whom Russian is the first foreign language. Quality is an important component of qualifications frameworks because, at least within the EHEA, quality assurance agencies will assess the quality of institutions with a view to the qualifications framework within which a given institution provides its qualifications and, conversely, qualifications will not be included in the framework if the institution providing them has not successfully undergone a quality assurance process.

Learning outcomes may be generic or subject specific. Generic learning outcomes, such as communication skills, the ability to reason in abstract terms, or aptitude for working both as part of a team and individually, are those that may be expected from any higher education graduate at a given level, irrespective of his or her field of study. Subject-specific learning outcomes, on the other hand, are, as the name indicates, specific to a given discipline: what a historian knows, understands and is able to do with relation to history or a chemist with relation to chemistry. Generic learning outcomes are included in the description of qualifications frameworks, whereas subject-specific learning outcomes are normally not. There may, however, be descriptions of subject-specific learning outcomes agreed by institutions or by the discipline community[48] that are not a part of the national qualifications framework, but that may nevertheless be valuable guides to what, say, the holder of a second degree in linguistics will know, understand and be able to do in relation to this discipline.

National and overarching frameworks

As we have already hinted at, qualifications frameworks may be one of two kinds: national or overarching.

National qualifications frameworks should perhaps more accurately be called system-specific frameworks, since they describe the qualifications in a given education or higher education system and since, as in the case of Belgium or the United Kingdom, one country may have more than one education system. Most often, however, one country has one education system, and we will stick to the term "national" with the caveat that the term also covers cases where a country has more than one education system.

National qualifications frameworks, then, describe all the qualifications in an education system, if the framework is comprehensive, or in a higher education system, if we are faced with a higher education qualifications framework. Whereas Australia, New Zealand and South Africa developed comprehensive frameworks, developments in Europe have been more mixed: some countries are seeking to develop comprehensive frameworks while others opt to develop higher education frameworks, which may be supplemented by a more comprehensive framework later. It would even be possible for a country to comply with the QF-EHEA and the EQF-LLL by developing a higher education framework only. Within the Bologna Process, ministers have committed to developing frameworks for higher education, whereas the requirement with regard to the EQF-LLL is that countries reference their qualifications against the overarching framework. Even if this does not require a national qualifications framework, it seems reasonable to assume that the vast majority of countries will indeed develop national frameworks for other parts of their education

---

48. The Tuning project (Tuning educational structures in Europe) provides a series of examples of subject-specific learning outcomes agreed by representatives of disciplines from several European countries, see http://tuning.unideusto.org/tuningeu/.

system too. One reason for the latter option may be that even if higher education qualifications may seem complex, they are considerably less complex that vocational qualifications, and there are also stronger international precedents in higher education.

As noted, all members of the Bologna Process have committed to developing national qualifications frameworks by 2012. Developing a national framework is a relatively complicated process that takes time. The Bologna Co-ordination Group on Qualifications Frameworks has outlined 11 steps, which are not to be taken as mandatory, nor are they necessarily to be accomplished in the order outlined by the group, but they give an indication of what is involved.

1. Decision to start: taken by the national body responsible for higher education.

2. Setting the agenda: the purpose of our national qualifications framework.

3. Organising the process: identifying stakeholders; setting up a committee/ working group.

4. Design profile: level structure, level descriptors (learning outcomes), credit ranges.

5. Consultation: national discussion and acceptance of design by stakeholders.

6. Approval according to national tradition by minister/government/legislation.

7. Administrative set-up: division of tasks of implementation between higher education institutions, the quality assurance agency and other bodies.

8. Implementation at institutional/programme level; reformulation of individual study programmes to learning outcome-based approach.

9. Inclusion of qualifications in the national qualifications framework; accredit-ation or similar.

10. Self-certification of compatibility with the EHEA framework (alignment to Bologna cycles, etc.).

11. Establishing a dedicated web page aimed at national stakeholders, as well as international partners (this step, in particular, should be accomplished as early as possible in the process and the website should be updated and developed as work on the national framework progresses).

As of August 2009, six national frameworks had been self-certified against the QF-EHEA: those of Belgium (Flemish Community), Germany, Ireland, the Netherlands, the United Kingdom (England, Wales and Northern Ireland) and the United Kingdom (Scotland). The other members of the Bologna Process are at various stages in the development of their national frameworks, and a survey carried out by the Bologna Co-ordination Group on Qualifications Frameworks in early 2009 showed that while more than 30 countries had completed the first three steps and some 25 had completed steps four and five, around 15 countries had already completed steps six and seven (Bologna Co-ordination Group on Qualifications Frameworks, 2009 a and b). However, developments are now relatively rapid and if a similar survey were undertaken in early 2010, it would most likely show that a considerably larger number of countries are well advanced in the process.

In addition to the three pioneering countries – Australia, New Zealand and South Africa – many countries outside the EHEA have developed or are developing qualifications frameworks. Malaysia has an established framework overseen by a qualifications authority, Thailand is well underway, some Canadian provinces have established provincial frameworks, and in the United States discussions on developing a framework have been cautiously launched. These are only select examples, since developments now seem to be so rapid that even if anything like a complete overview were established, it would most likely be outdated before publication. Qualifications frameworks have very much become part of the global discourse, and increasingly also part of the global practice, of higher education reform.[49]

It is important to note that there may well be several qualifications located at the same level within a national framework. If level one denotes a first cycle qualification, there may be different kinds of such qualifications that are all at the same level in the national qualifications frameworks, but that may have slightly different characteristics. As an example, level six in the Irish qualifications framework comprises two distinct qualifications that the Irish framework describes as follows:

Level 6 Advanced Certificate

What is this?

An Advanced Certificate award enables development of a variety of skills which may be vocationally specific and/or of a general supervisory nature. The majority of Level 6 holders take up positions of employment. A Certificate holder at this level may also transfer to a programme leading to the next level of the framework.

Example

An example of awards at Level 6 includes Advanced Certificate Craft-Electrical.

Awarding Body

The awarding body for this award is the Further Education and Training Awards Council (FETAC).

---

49. This was demonstrated by a conference on the global dimension of qualifications frameworks organised by the European Training Foundation in January 2009, see www.etf.europa.eu/web.nsf/opennews/AA73545A989E34FAC12575520053DFA5_EN?OpenDocument.

Level 6 Higher Certificate

What is this?

The Higher Certificate is normally awarded after completion of a programme of two years duration in a recognised higher education institution. A Certificate holder at this level may transfer to a programme on the next level of the framework.

Example

An example of awards at Level 6 Higher Certificate is a Certificate in Business Studies.

Awarding Body

The awarding bodies for this award is the Higher Education and Training Awards Council (HETAC) the Dublin Institute of Technology (DIT) and the Institutes of Technology (IOT).[50]

In terms of the QF-EHEA, both would be short cycle qualifications within the first cycle.

Where Europe has been truly innovative is with regard to overarching frameworks. These are more general than national frameworks and they set the parameters within which the relevant national frameworks will be developed. One way of seeing overarching qualifications frameworks is that they describe the outer limits within which national frameworks will be developed. Within these limits, there is scope for considerable variation that allows countries to take account of their own specific needs, strengths and traditions, but at the same time the overarching framework ensures that this variation between national frameworks is kept manageable. There is nothing to prevent a country from developing a national framework where the learning outcomes for a first degree are such that a typical student would need 10 years or more after completion of secondary school to obtain the qualification, but this would not be a national framework compatible with the QF-EHEA, nor would it be in accordance with the overall trends of higher education reform in other parts of the world. For the same reasons, the example is of course entirely fictitious.

As we have seen, the QF-EHEA was adopted by the ministers of the Bologna Process in 2005, and it applies to the 46 countries of the EHEA. As will be seen from the overview below, the QF-EHEA does not include a description of what have come to be described as "short cycle" qualifications. Typically, short cycle qualifications have a workload of approximately 120 ECTS credits – although some have more or less – and are a feature of professional higher education. In the United States, the Associate Degree would be an example of the kind of qualification that in Europe is often referred to as "short cycle". Short cycle qualifications are to be found in many countries, and the decision by the 2005 ministerial conference of the Bologna

---

50. www.nfq.ie/nfq/en/about_NFQ/framework_levels_award_types.html.

Process gave education systems the possibility of including intermediate qualifications within each of the three cycles of their national qualifications frameworks. It seems safe to assume that these will most often be short cycle qualifications within the first cycle.

The EHEA qualifications framework

	Outcomes	ECTS credits
First cycle qualification	Qualifications that signify completion of the first cycle are awarded to students who: – have demonstrated knowledge and understanding in a field of study that builds upon their general secondary education, and is typically at a level that, whilst supported by advanced textbooks, includes some aspects that will be informed by knowledge of the forefront of their field of study; – can apply their knowledge and understanding in a manner that indicates a professional approach to their work or vocation, and have competences typically demonstrated through devising and sustaining arguments and solving problems within their field of study; – have the ability to gather and interpret relevant data (usually within their field of study) to inform judgments that include reflection on relevant social, scientific or ethical issues; – can communicate information, ideas, problems and solutions to both specialist and non-specialist audiences; – have developed those learning skills that are necessary for them to continue to undertake further study with a high degree of autonomy.	Typically include 180-240 ECTS credits

	Outcomes	ECTS credits
Second cycle qualification	Qualifications that signify completion of the second cycle are awarded to students who: – have demonstrated knowledge and understanding that is founded upon and extends and/or enhances that typically associated with the first cycle, and that provides a basis or opportunity for originality in developing and/or applying ideas, often within a research context; – can apply their knowledge and understanding, and problem-solving abilities in new or unfamiliar environments within broader (or multidisciplinary) contexts related to their field of study; – have the ability to integrate knowledge and handle complexity, and formulate judgments with incomplete or limited information, but that include reflecting on social and ethical responsibilities linked to the application of their knowledge and judgments; – can communicate their conclusions, and the knowledge and rationale underpinning these, to specialist and non-specialist audiences clearly and unambiguously; – have the learning skills to allow them to continue to study in a manner that may be largely self-directed or autonomous.	Typically include 90-120 ECTS credits, with a minimum of 60 credits at the level of the second cycle
Third cycle qualification	Qualifications that signify completion of the third cycle are awarded to students who: – have demonstrated a systematic understanding of a field of study and mastery of the skills and methods of research associated with that field;	Not specified

	Outcomes	ECTS credits
	– have demonstrated the ability to conceive, design, implement and adapt a substantial process of research with scholarly integrity;	
	– have made a contribution through original research that extends the frontier of knowledge by developing a substantial body of work, some of which merits national or international refereed publication;	
	– are capable of critical analysis, evaluation and synthesis of new and complex ideas;	
	– can communicate with their peers, the larger scholarly community and with society in general about their areas of expertise;	
	– can be expected to be able to promote, within academic and professional contexts, technological, social or cultural advancement in a knowledge based society.	

As we have also seen, at approximately the same time that the QF-EHEA was adopted, the European Commission launched work on the European Qualifications Framework for lifelong learning (EQF-LLL), which was formally established in spring 2008.

To this author's knowledge, the QF-EHEA and the EQF-LLL are the only existing examples of overarching qualifications frameworks. There are, however, discussions within the Gulf Cooperation Council about a possible overarching framework for this region, which encompasses Bahrain, Kuwait, Oman, Qatar, Saudi Arabia and the United Arab Emirates. As the Bologna Process is considered with interest as a possible inspiration (much more than a model to be copied for higher education in other areas of the world, one might imagine that overarching frameworks may in time be developed for, or within, some other regions. In addition, one might imagine that some federal states might opt for national frameworks with characteristics close to those of overarching frameworks, which would serve to ensure that provincial or state frameworks develop coherently.

Even if much of the European debate has focused on the overarching frameworks, it is the national qualifications frameworks that are closest to the daily lives of learners. The relationship between national and overarching frameworks may be summarised as follows:

National frameworks	Overarching frameworks
– closest to the operational reality	– facilitate movement between systems
– owned by national system	– are the face of qualifications from the region (for example, EHEA) to the rest of the world
– ultimately determine what qualifications learners will earn	
– describe the qualifications within a given education system and how they interlink	– provide the broad structure within which national qualifications frameworks will be developed ("outer limits" for diversity)

As we have seen, the QF-EHEA is specific to higher education, while the EQF-LLL is comprehensive. This implies that they share a set of qualifications, namely those pertaining to higher education. It may therefore be argued that Europe has two distinct overarching frameworks for higher education, at least as concerns the 32 countries of the EQF-LLL, all of which are also party to the QF-EHEA. In a formal sense, this is true and the two frameworks do not describe the higher education qualifications in exactly the same terms. However, the descriptions are similar and, most importantly, it is entirely possible to develop national qualifications frameworks for higher education that are compatible with both overarching frameworks.

Self-certification

Self-certification has been developed as a concept within the EHEA and the discussion here will therefore be confined to national frameworks compatible with the QF-EHEA. Within the EQF-LL, referencing is a similar process with criteria largely modelled on those for self-certification within the QF-EHEA.

Self-certification is the final step in the development of national qualifications frameworks and it is the means through which the competent public authorities convince their international partners that their national framework is compatible with the QF-EHEA. Countries are sovereign with full authority over their education systems and no international body can certify a national framework in lieu of the competent national authority. However, self-certification is not a question only of formal authority but also of legitimacy, acceptance and the creation of trust. A country that published a statement simply saying its national framework is certified as compatible with the QF-EHEA could not be obliged to change its statement in formal terms, but it is unlikely such a statement would convince partners inside or outside the EHEA and it would therefore be of little benefit to the country concerned. In such a case, which is likely to remain fictitious, peer pressure would probably be applied in very considerable doses.

The self-certification report may be considered as the "visiting card" of the national qualifications framework concerned; it is the one document through which the competent authorities will demonstrate, through reasoned arguments according to agreed criteria, that their framework is compatible. This has strong implications for recognition, because if a national framework is convincingly self-certified as "QF-EHEA compatible", it will be much less likely that there are substantial differences between this framework and other similar frameworks.

While the scope of this article does not allow us to explore the criteria and procedure for self-certification in detail,[51] it is worth underlining that one of the requirements agreed to by ministers is that there be involvement by foreign experts in the selfcertification process. This adds credibility and improves transparency, and it is also useful because foreigners may question elements of a framework that may be self-explanatory to those intimately familiar with it, but may require explanation to outsiders. Self-certification reports are normally developed by a group composed of national and foreign experts and then adopted by the competent national authorities. It is then published on the Bologna website[52] as well as on the ENIC/NARIC website,[53] so that all completed reports are easily accessible.

Qualifications frameworks and recognition

The answer to the question asked in the title of this article – Are qualifications frameworks a useful instrument to resolve substantial differences? – is a "yes, but…". Seen from a recognition point of view, a qualifications framework is above all a transparency instrument. A qualifications framework should make it easier to determine whether a foreign qualification ought to be recognised, or whether there are substantial differences between this qualification and similar qualifications in the country in which recognition is sought. In particular, a qualifications framework should help answer any questions pertaining to level, quality assurance, workload (to the extent that this is a relevant question for recognition) and generic learning outcomes, as well as the functions of a given qualification in terms of access to further studies and possibly to the labour market in its country of origin. Qualifications frameworks are, as we have seen, less likely to answer questions pertaining to profile or subject-specific learning outcomes. In answering this set of questions, qualifications frameworks have the potential both to reduce the workload of credentials evaluators and to reduce the elements of a qualification on which substantial differences might possibly exist. While it may be possible to consider that the profile of two qualifications at a similar level in two different qualifications framework may constitute a substantial difference for certain purposes of recognition, it would be much more difficult to argue that there are similar differences in terms of level, quality, workload or generic learning outcomes if both frameworks have been

---

51. For further details, see www.ond.vlaanderen.be/hogeronderwijs/bologna/qf/documents/Bologna_Framework_and_Certification_revised_29_02_08.pdf.
52. See www.ond.vlaanderen.be/hogeronderwijs/bologna/qf/national.asp#C.
53. See www.enic-naric.net/index.aspx?s=n&r=ena&d=qf.

self-certified against the QF-EHEA. In this case, the argument would in fact need to be that the self-certification report as published is unconvincing, which would be a strong indictment of the competent public authorities as well as of the foreign experts who have participated in the self-certification.

Qualifications frameworks should therefore be of considerable help in furthering fair recognition, as required by the Lisbon Recognition Convention, but it is important to underline that they are not some kind of magic formula to solve all recognition problems. They should facilitate the assessment of individual qualifications, but they will not make such an assessment superfluous, nor will they lead to "automatic recognition". While it may be assumed that first degrees from two different national frameworks self-certified against the QF-EHEA will be of similar level, quality, workload and generic learning outcomes, an assessment will still need to be undertaken and, for some purposes of recognition, it will most likely also include profile and subject-specific learning outcomes.

At the same time, as underlined in the introduction to this article, the absence of a national or overarching qualifications framework cannot be construed as a substantial difference in itself. In the present state of affairs, this would imply that only qualifications from six higher education systems within the EHEA should be recognised, and these would be supplemented by qualifications from a limited number of countries outside the EHEA. A national qualifications framework is an instrument that furthers recognition but it is not a requirement. Many countries inside and outside the EHEA are in the process of developing their frameworks, or are discussing whether to do so, but a number of countries may ultimately decide not to do so, or even debate whether this is the right direction to take. This does not render their qualifications any less valuable. Qualifications frameworks will help recognition, but the absence of qualifications frameworks should not make recognition any more difficult in the future than it has been in the past, before qualifications frameworks came into existence. Qualifications frameworks or not, credentials evaluators will need to use the transparency instruments they have at their disposal, gather the required information and make their decisions, with due regard to international and national regulations and guidelines, but without leaving aside the element of decision making that is impossible to describe in legal terms: common sense.

References

Association of American Colleges and Universities, *College Learning for the New Global Century*, AAC&U, Washington DC, 2007.

Bergan, S., "Public responsibility for higher education and research: what does it mean?", in Weber, L. and Bergan, S. (eds), *Public Responsibility for Higher Education and Research*, Council of Europe Higher Education Series No. 2, Council of Europe Publishing, Strasbourg, 2005.

Bergan, S., *Qualifications. Introduction to a Concept,* Council of Europe Higher Education Series No. 6, Council of Europe Publishing, Strasbourg, 2007.

Bologna Co-ordination Group on Qualifications Frameworks, *Report on Qualifications Frameworks*, Strasbourg/Brussels: Bologna Process and Council of Europe, 2009a. Available at: www.ond.vlaanderen.be/hogeronderwijs/bologna/ conference/documents/2009_QF_CG_report.pdf.

Bologna Co-ordination Group on Qualifications Frameworks, *Synthesis of the replies received from national QF correspondents*, Strasbourg/Brussels: Bologna Process and Council of Europe, 2009b. Available at: www.ond.vlaanderen.be/ hogeronderwijs/bologna/conference/documents/Synthesis_NQF_Reports_ March2009.pdf.

Council of Europe Recommendation Rec(2007)6 of the Committee of Ministers to member states on the public responsibility for higher education and research, 2007.

IV. Conclusion

Applying the Lisbon recognition principles to the question of substantial difference: what have we learned?

E. Stephen Hunt

The research, case studies and policy discussions contained in this book demonstrate the complexity and subtlety of the issues surrounding substantial difference. Over several years of case studies, survey research and focusing on the routine work of ENICs and NARICs, the Working Party on Substantial Differences has endeavoured to operationally define what substantial difference means to national competent authorities and to develop general suggestions concerning good practices. The current volume seeks to tie all this together, and this article tries to summarise what has been learned from three sources: (1) theory: as derived from the Lisbon Recognition Convention and subsidiary texts; (2) empirical evidence from the NARIC survey and case studies; and (3) the suggested good practices that may result from the research.

Theoretical principles of substantial difference policy

In the first chapter – "Substantial differences: exploring a concept" – Sjur Bergan has provided a thorough review of how substantial difference is used in the Lisbon Recognition Convention, the explanatory report and related texts developed via the Bologna Process. The explanatory report suggests four possible examples of substantial difference, each of which deserves clarification and updating in the context of developments since the mid-1990s.

General versus specialised technical education has, since 1996, been clarified so that "general" is understood to mean any kind of academic education, in any subject or subjects at different levels, that does not specifically prepare a student to enter a technical or professional field or a trade. It has become increasingly obvious, as the Bologna ministerial conferences and the Bologna Follow-Up Group have defined the degree cycles and the expected outcomes, that non-technical and non-professional subjects at the secondary, short cycle, or first cycle levels are not really specialised in the sense of the explanatory report. Secondary qualifications that give access to tertiary education are now more varied than a decade ago, and clear policy lines exist in many countries that encourage seamless access for qualified students from secondary school, through short cycle programmes, to the initial level of higher education. Furthermore, the first cycle qualification is intended to prepare students equally for the labour market or further studies, and is not supposed to merely be the first portion of a traditional "long cycle" programme. Competence in the degree subject is certainly expected, but not at a master's level (second cycle). To interpret contemporary qualifications earned in general academic subjects at the first cycle level or below as technically specialised is not a logical approach, not-withstanding the historical idea that a university degree (in long cycle days) signi-fied professional-level subject mastery. Likewise, to negatively assess first cycle qualifications that require and contain generalist competencies (related subjects, unrelated subjects, interpersonal and job market skills, and so on) on the grounds that these cannot compare to "pure" single subject qualifications is also less com-mon than in the past. (This is much to the relief of holders of the French *licence*, Francophone *licences*, and North American or Japanese bachelor's degrees, among others.)

Length, although mentioned in the explanatory report, is now almost universally ignored as a substantial difference factor, unless the variations in the relative length of studies are so extreme as to call into question issues of level, content, quality and outcomes. And even then, length is less likely to be a primary factor than the other substantive issues. The only residual area where length is a factor tends to be in unreformed credentials evaluation practices and in narrowly regulated profes-sional licence requirements. Neither of these is, by general consensus, an example of best practices. This is a significant development: as late as the early to mid-1990s, several European countries expressed concern over secondary school leaving quali-fications from central and eastern European countries (then referred to as "new member countries") because, in many cases, these countries had 11- rather than 12-year systems of primary and secondary education. Today, these arguments are rarely heard.

The distribution and amount of specified subjects remains a generally accepted factor in substantial difference analyses if the issue relates to actual concentration requirements (either an academic or professional field), or if it relates to counting credits at lower level as valid for a higher level. In both cases the distribution and amount of specified subjects need to be relevant to purpose for which recognition is sought. For example, undergraduate (first cycle) subjects that must be completed as prerequisites for undertaking graduate-level studies are not generally considered part of the higher degree requirements. And it remains accepted – with caveats – that subject concentration requirements should be met (including any thesis or practical requirements) in order for home or host qualifications to be considered comparable in content, particularly in professional fields. Where experience has tended to modify distribution and amount requirements is with the advent of outcomes-based evaluation. If the Lisbon principles of considering the purpose for which recognition is sought and the function of a qualification are followed, then it becomes important not to rely on narrow analyses of the curricular content of a qualification or period of study, but rather to assess its inputs and outcomes. The empirical evidence to be discussed below clearly shows that the issue of the distri-bution and amount of subjects has undergone change since the explanatory report was drafted, and no longer implies that variations in content are necessarily sub-stantial differences.

The focus of a qualification, the fourth example cited in the explanatory report, has also undergone change since the 1990s. This consideration referred to whether the focus of the awarding institution, or faculty or programme, was considered primarily to prepare students for work or for further academic study. The core principle remains valid, especially in clear cases of vocational versus academic focuses where level is also an issue. Terminal, short cycle vocational training, or training for which credit cannot be assessed, is unlikely to be considered comparable to technical, professional or academic studies at the higher education level. Beyond this rather extreme case, however, much of the differentiation that was valid over a decade ago is no longer so clear-cut. For example, the historical distinction between "university" and "non-university" higher education has become blurred, as countries modify their national systems to promote access, develop new policies on credit transfer and bridging between types and levels of education, and even in some cases eliminate most or all of the university/non-university distinctions as a matter of law. The Bologna action line on lifelong learning and the European Commission's policies in this area now call for work to promote better access between vocational, adult and academic education. Even at the secondary leaving level, there are now more opportunities to gain access to tertiary education than in the past. And the qualifications frameworks that are now part of the EHEA (as well as other policies elsewhere) call for preparation for non-academic as well as academic work at all three degree levels. Focus remains a useful concept in principle, but it is no longer easy to determine a substantial difference just by noting the name or type of institution, the name of a qualification or the kind of educational experience.

Other important principles can be derived from the Lisbon Recognition Convention and its subsidiary texts. Among the most important, and worthy of quoting again, is this:

> [T]he difference must be both substantial and relevant as defined by the competent recognition authority. Recognition cannot be withheld for reasons immaterial to the qualification or the purpose for which recognition is sought (*Explanatory report, Article VI.1)*

Factors which are irrelevant to the qualification in question, or the purpose an applicant has in requesting recognition, should never intrude upon the recognition analysis or decision. If the competent recognition authority has rules defining what is expected in a qualification eligible for recognition for a specific purpose, then these must be respected, since the host country has the right to determine eligibility. However, even in this area there are certain types of criteria which are considered more or less acceptable than others, as will been seen from the following discussion.

Additional basic principles may be stated as follows:

–   If a genuine substantial difference can be shown, then it may be possible or necessary to grant only partial recognition or to deny recognition.

– The burden of proof in establishing that a substantial difference exists falls on the competent recognition authority, not on the applicant or – by extension – the institution originally awarding the credits or qualification, or the system in which it resides.

– Even if a substantial difference exists, this does not entail an obligation to consider it, or to reject a qualification. Competent recognition authorities may choose to ignore even a substantial difference if other factors are considered to outweigh it. Such instances might be rare, but could involve mutual recognition agreements, evidence of subsequent performance, or other factors.

– Excessively narrow nostrification, equivalence or "bean-counting" analyses should not outweigh consideration of the function of a qualification and the purpose for which recognition is sought. Two identical educational qualifications from different systems do not exist, and even qualifications earned within the same system, or by different students in an institution, often show variation. Essential core requirements cannot be ignored, but mobility should not be endangered through narrow, restrictive or protectionist requirements that ignore the principles of recognition, the natural diversity within and among European or global systems, or the goal of promoting mobility.

– Periods of study undertaken in different countries en route to a qualification are to be afforded recognition where possible (Article V.1) and are not to be considered a barrier to recognition unless a genuine substantial difference can be shown. The EHEA, the EU and UNESCO all clearly promote short-term academic mobility, including in dissimilar systems. Nor is the fact that a student studied overseas on his or her own, rather than as part of an official programme, to be considered a substantial difference (Explanatory report, Article V.1).

– While qualifications or credits earned from non-recognised institutions can constitute a substantial difference, competent recognition authorities should refer to the principles outlined in the paper "Qualifications from Non-Recognized Institutions: An Overview of the Issue", which was adopted by the ENIC/NARIC networks in 2008 (cf. this author's article on the topic in the present volume). Qualifications from bogus providers or substandard institutions usually result in a substantial difference issue, but qualifications from legitimate non-recognised institutions (government, military, religious, adult and some pre-Bologna programmes) usually do not.

– As with all other recognition procedures and decisions, those involving substantial difference issues should be communicated to applicants in a timely manner and some form of appeal should be provided.

The empirical evidence

As has been shown, the principles inherent in the Lisbon Recognition Convention and its subsidiary texts have sometimes been modified over time by historical developments and the practical experience of competent recognition authorities.

Practitioners often have a general idea of what prevailing professional ideas towards recognition are and how these change, but the press of work and the lack of systematic analysis often leaves their views in the anecdotal stage. The Working Party on Substantial Differences undertook two projects to address the need for empirical evidence of recognition practices in general and attitudes/policies towards substantial difference in particular. The first of these was a series of structured case studies presented to the ENIC and NARIC networks over the period 2006-08. In these case studies, ENIC Network members were asked to react to fact patterns in specific fictitious case presentations and provide responses – these are included in Part II of this book. At the same time, during the period 2007-08, the European Commission funded a survey of the recognition practices among NARIC centres that involved a structured analysis of responses to actual cases. This project was headed by Bas Wegewijs and Lucie de Bruin of NUFFIC in the Netherlands, and their findings appear in Part III. The results of these empirical studies are very informative for mapping the current state of practice with respect to substantial difference and for pointing to areas of convergence and change.

Broadly speaking, the most important result of these research efforts is to reveal the objective existence of two broad recognition approaches as posited by Sjur Bergan in his article on the "two cultures" of recognition: (1) a legalistic, predominantly bureaucratic approach based on strict fidelity to often narrow rules, attention to equivalence analyses and policies that respect legal formalities above all other forms of evidence, and (2) an approach that respects regulations and policies but that affords competent recognition authorities the discretion to mitigate rules in the light of other evidence and that puts emphasis on the function of a qualification and the purpose for which recognition is sought, rather than strict adherence to equivalence formulae. There is little doubt, based on the NARIC survey, that the prevailing mode of thinking within the competent recognition authorities inside the EU tends towards the legalistic. In the words of the survey authors:

> A striking conclusion of this survey *is that, in virtually all cases, the formal rights of the qualification in the sending country seem to prevail over any other argument. This may lead to a* stricter *or a more* lenient outcome as compared to the evaluations based on learning outcomes. In that sense, there is no clear relationship between reliance on formal, legalistic arguments and the strictness of the [recognition] outcome. Still, the legalistic approach does not always seem to be favourable from the point of view of the holder of the qualification, as it seems to produce more mismatches between the competencies of the student [applicant for recognition] and the competencies required for entrance into a particular programme. If the student [applicant] has the right competencies but is rejected on formal grounds, cross-border mobility is directly hindered. If the student [applicant] is admitted to a programme [due to meeting formalistic criteria] but is lacking in some essential competence(s), the student is not likely to enjoy a fruitful mobility experience. (*Wegewijs and de Bruin, 2009,* present volume*)*

It is perhaps not surprising that an objective survey of NARIC practices reveals a tendency to rely on legalistic formalities rather than the less structured evidence of learning outcomes and competencies. Like many competent recognition authorities around the world, nearly every ENIC/NARIC office is a government agency. Public offices connected to ministries or other large bureaucratic authorities – whether in the United States, Europe, or anywhere else, as Max Weber established in the late 19th century – are creatures of rules and rely on them, as they must, to achieve both objectivity and equity. Legally accountable government agencies cannot substitute their own experience, knowledge or sympathies for the law, unless the law expressly permits such discretion. And discretion is usually circumscribed because of the need to avoid crossing the fine line between documentable and defensible exceptions and mitigations, on the one hand, and more subjective judgments that could expose an agency to lawsuits, on the other.

What is equally interesting about the case studies and the NARIC survey, however, is the observation that most professional staff in the NARICs and ENICs believe that a less legalistic and more outcomes-based approach is preferable to that which they currently follow. Indeed, there is some evidence from comments received from the case study respondents that they are working to get restrictive requirements revised and, in some cases, expect more liberal discretionary rules to be forthcoming. This is good news for recognition and for dealing with the issue of substantial difference.

It is possible to briefly summarise the outcomes of the case study and survey exercises, as these add further context to developing a sense of good practices with respect to substantial difference.

– Institutional characteristics are generally irrelevant (name, type, university/ non-university, etc.), as are names of programmes and titles per se. Other factors, such as level, accreditation, core content requirements, and so on are much more important.

– The system or country of origin is irrelevant and should not be an argument for substantial difference, as this rarely, if ever, has anything to do with the issues of function or purpose and introduces indefensible bias that could also violate formal agreements and laws. Some ENICs and NARICs acknowledge that this problem exists, but all agree that it is bad practice to rely on national impressions and biases in making recognition decisions that are subject to appeal.

– Likewise, studying at different institutions en route to a qualification, and in different systems, is irrelevant (per the convention) and should not be a factor in recognition decisions. ENICs and NARICs did acknowledge, however, that some prejudice against this exists, notwithstanding EHEA, EU, Council of Europe and UNESCO policy,[54] and it needs to be combated.

---

54. See also the Recommendation on the Recognition on Joint Degrees adopted by the Lisbon Recognition Convention Committee in 2004, available at: https://wcd.coe.int/com.instranet. InstraServlet?command=com.instranet.CmdBlobGet&InstranetImage=320284&SecMode=1&DocId=822138&Usage=2.

– The presence of non-academic elements in a programme or qualification may or may not be a substantial difference factor, depending on the function of the qualification and the purpose for which recognition is sought. Internships and other practicums, for example, may be positive elements in a professional or vocational qualification, but irrelevant or negative in other types of qualifications.

– Features such as length, number of credits, or number of contact hours are irrelevant unless other issues, such as level, quality or core content requirements are affected.

– It helps to have some information about learning outcomes, either in a Diploma Supplement or other description of the function of a qualification in the home system, and the complete absence of any information about the qualification can become a recognition issue.

– It is perfectly acceptable in practice to request additional information from an applicant or from another source.

– It is difficult to correctly deal with qualifications for which it is impossible to estimate credit, either directly or indirectly via some conversion formula. This could be a potential issue with respect to adult learning outcomes or other forms of learning that lie outside the formal academic context.

– Accreditation or some other form of quality assurance is important, but the type of accreditation or quality assurance (institutional, programmatic, etc.) is not as important as that it exists, covers the qualification or credits in question, and has some appropriate recognition inside the home system.

– The level of a qualification can be a substantial difference factor, but it is wise to consider whether the issue of level is legalistic (that is, what the home country called the level at the time the qualification was issued) or whether the outcomes and competencies indicate that the holder can or cannot be reasonably expected to meet host country requirements for recognition, given the purpose for which he/she requests recognition.

– Legal licensure requirements are important and can trump educational considerations, especially if the purpose for which recognition is sought is to obtain a work permit or permission to practise a regulated profession or trade.

– Agreement by home and host country competent professional authorities on the acceptability of a qualification to satisfy work or licensure requirements can be a positive factor that helps the recognition process, even if other questions exist.

– Requirements, including directives, specific to the EHEA or EU member states cannot be imposed upon qualifications and their issuing systems outside of the EHEA and EU unless the purpose for which recognition is sought involves an activity that subjects the applicant to EHEA or EU regulations, such as working inside Europe. For example, denying a non-European qualification recognition because there is no national qualifications framework, no Diploma

Supplement, the degree structure is not Bologna-compliant or the national quality assurance process is not listed in a European registry are not, per se, grounds for invoking a substantial difference issue.

– Conversely, requirements and directives specific to the EHEA or EU can be used to raise substantial difference arguments if the home system of an applicant is in a country that is a member of the EHEA or EU, is not exempt from the provision in question, but the qualification or practice is not compliant with applicable intra-European rules.

– Requiring proof of a valid work permit prior to granting recognition of a professional or vocational qualification is an unrealistic and unfair practice, because it puts the cart before the horse – in nearly all countries a work visa or permit cannot be issued by a consulate, immigration or labour office without a credentials evaluation stating that the applicant's education or training is satisfactory for the purpose for which the permit or visa is sought.

– Likewise, requiring proof of citizenship or permanent residence, in a specific country or in the EU, is not a good recognition practice. This is protectionist and effectively denies recognition on the basis of nationality.

The above list of actual practices demonstrates that competent recognition authorities in the European Region are very conscious of the need to restrict the issue of substantial difference to cases where recognition is problematic. It shows that – despite the need to adhere to some legalistic restrictions – most competent recognition authorities are determined to make positive decisions wherever possible and are consciously avoiding erecting unnecessary barriers to recognition. The empirical studies show that the professional consensus across Europe is to use as much discretion as the law makes available and to promote practices that make European recognition fair and straightforward for holders of European and non-European qualifications. At the same time, this evidence indicates that competent recognition authorities are aware of the applicability of European directives inside the EU and EHEA, but are also trying to be careful not to impose these requirements outside Europe in ways that would adversely affect recognition in a global context and international mobility. There are still situations in which narrowly restrictive regulations affect recognition, especially in the regulated professions and trades. The author can attest, however, to the fact that narrow and restrictive professional recognition policies are a universal problem and by no means peculiar to the European Region. As the reality of globalisation puts pressure on the professions themselves to permit freer rules for professional mobility, this situation will change. It is already happening in the health and engineering professions, as well as accountancy, and is beginning to be discussed in the legal profession. When the professions acknowledge the need for mobility, their associations in turn lobby legislatures to modify formerly restrictive rules, and this in turn provides greater flexibility to the competent recognition authorities.

Towards good practices

Examination of the primary documents pertaining to recognition, and the practices prevailing among competent recognition authorities, are necessary first steps in developing suggestions for good practices in the area of substantial difference. There are a few other factors that deserve attention before summarising the current and desired state of affairs with respect to substantial difference.

The global dimension

It is important, when addressing substantial difference in the context of the Lisbon Recognition Convention and its subsidiary documents, to recognise that the European Region, and the wider world, take in far more than simply the EHEA or the European Union. While this is an obvious statement, it is not always realised in practice. The importance of developing the EHEA; of implementing the Bologna reforms; developing European qualifications frameworks as well as national frameworks compatible with these and promoting academic, professional, vocational and adult mobility in the European context are high priorities for the majority of European Region countries belonging to the EU and/or the EHEA. These priorities, while international in the sense that these countries are completely sovereign with respect to educational matters, are in another sense "domestic" in the context of intra-European affairs, as well as the fact that the EU and EHEA areas share a common heritage. Legislation, regulations, policies and practices intended to satisfy European agreements and commitments can inadvertently erect barriers to international mobility and recognition from outside the EHEA if their design and implementation create requirements or expectations that non-EHEA systems, institutions and their graduates cannot reasonably meet. Since the global dimension is now a Bologna action line, and there is a concerted effort both to attract students to Europe and to export European education and research globally, globally sensitive recognition policies are called for as never before.

The Communiqué adopted unanimously by the UNESCO World Conference on Higher Education in Paris on 8 July 2009 is a good place to start (UNESCO, ED.2009/CONF.402/2). It contains several key observations that are critical for promoting good recognition practices across the diverse kinds of educational systems, providers and challenges facing educators today.

–   Higher education is a public good (paragraph 1), but there are many stakeholders in addition to governments, and institutions can legitimately have different missions (paragraph 5), and can be legitimately public or private (paragraphs 10, 35).

–   Distance learning can be a positive boon to access, quality, and good outcomes (paragraphs 14-18).

–   Transnational or cross-border education providers and arrangements can be a positive development if properly quality-assured (paragraph 28), and if diploma mills and frauds are effectively dealt with (paragraph 29).

–   International co-operation and cross-border inter-institutional and faculty partnerships are a definite good and to be encouraged (paragraphs 25 and 31-34).

–   Educational systems and institutions should ensure comprehensive access and opportunity from vocational education through advanced research, including adult/lifelong education, entrepreneurship (commercial or business) education and higher education (paragraphs 19, 22).

–   Effective national quality assurance mechanisms are essential (paragraph 27), as is international co-operation among them.

–   In developing international co-operation and quality assurance, it is critical to promote access and opportunity, promote quality, and respect both cultural diversity and national sovereignty (paragraph 26).

The communiqué also emphasised the importance of capacity building and co-operation with less-developed countries, with a special emphasis on Africa, and on the need for innovative and flexible curricula emphasising technology, science and socially relevant studies.

What this means for recognition is that the global community has now clearly declared that the days of conservative, traditionalist, elitist and compartmentalised education are coming to a close. It means that equality of educational access and opportunity is a universal priority, regardless of whether students are traditional-age or adult; whether delivery is via traditional institutions, distance learning or trans-national institutions, and without restrictions according to gender, origin, religion, race, ethnicity, disability or status. And it has also answered a long-standing debate by declaring unequivocally that there is nothing wrong with a public good being delivered by private providers as well as by non-traditional (electronic, adult, cross-border) means. The essential cross-cutting element making all this possible will be good quality assurance provided by national quality assurance authorities who co-operate internationally. And the social imperative will be to promote effective public/private, cross-border, inter-institutional and faculty partnerships; student and faculty exchanges; co-operative research; outreach to developing countries needing capacity-building; and to assure access and opportunity for all, regardless of their backgrounds or the type of study (adult, vocational, private, distance, commercial, traditional university, transnational, interdisciplinary, etc.) in which they begin their academic careers.

A UNESCO conference resolution is, of course, a non-binding document, and many national systems, including within and outside the European Region, are far away from the educational flexibility and progressivism envisioned in the communiqué. Nevertheless, the signals are clear. Recognition authorities who labour under rules, or choose to adopt practices, that frown upon flexibility, innovation and different approaches to similar situations, are going to become increasing beleaguered, and conservative legalistic approaches may cause national systems to fall behind in attracting international students, developing research and other co-operative enterprises, forming partnerships, and exporting their graduates and services.

Current European developments

Reform and change are now endemic to the EHEA and the emerging European Research Area (ERA). Not only has the Bologna Process radically transformed European higher education; it is rapidly being matched by the progress at the post-secondary vocational level, via the Copenhagen Process. Over the past couple of decades, national systems have been modified to introduce credit systems and the Diploma Supplement, create new or modified degree and other qualification structures, develop qualifications frameworks, end long-standing transfer barriers between university and non-university tertiary education, permit the international transportability of student assistance funds, and establish networks of competent recognition authorities and information centres.

— Where Europe once saw itself as a victim of transnational education and global competition, many European countries today are themselves exporters of education services and many European institutions operate branch campuses, or provide distance learning in the Middle East, Asia-Pacific, Africa, Latin America and even North America. The Code of Good Practice in the Provision of Transnational Education was first adopted by the ENIC and NARIC networks in 2000, revised in 2007, and is now widely accepted as the principal international guide for permitting legitimate cross-border education to exist.

— Distance learning, which was still viewed with much suspicion when the Lisbon Recognition Convention was being negotiated in 1996, is now an accepted method of providing tertiary education and nearly every EHEA country has at least one recognised open or distance institution in its own system.

— In 1996, when this author began his work as manager of an ENIC centre, there were countries within the European Region which refused to recognise the MBA as a degree; whose systems did not permit graduates of non-university tertiary education to continue their studies and transfer to universities without severe penalties or starting over; where transnational and distance education were viewed as irredeemable threats to the public good; where private provision of tertiary education was prohibited or severely restricted; and where interdisciplinary studies, joint degrees, consortia, credit transfer and mutual recognition were foreign concepts. Nearly all of this has changed.

— Today, the European University Association is recommending an interdisciplinary and flexible European Doctorate for the third cycle qualification. Educators are coming to realise that the new first cycle bachelor's degrees are not simply the first half of an old long cycle qualification, but must incorporate the subject flexibility to enable holders to function in the job market whether they continue their studies or not. And the formerly all-but-forgotten short cycle qualification level of less than three years is now being rediscovered as a useful means to institutionalise the bridge between vocational and higher education and give citizens truly seamless access and opportunity.

These developments are often being paralleled elsewhere than in the European Region. In Australia and New Zealand, innovative national systems have emerged that use quite different concepts of qualifications frameworks and accountability to those prevailing in Europe, but equally effective ones. Canadian provinces and US states have developed (Ontario) or are actively exploring (United States) the development of their own versions of qualifications frameworks (in the US case, with Bologna experts invited to advise educational authorities in co-operating states). A healthy debate has arisen inside the United States with respect to the need to modernise US credentials evaluation practices, and the Higher Education Opportunities Act of 2009 adopts clearer policies for access across all educational and qualification levels, and ensures credit transfer among all institutions accredited by recognised agencies, regardless of whether the agency is regional or national. These external systems and their developments do not resemble those in the EHEA, but there is no requirement for them to do so. As Sjur Bergan emphasises in "Approaches to recognition: a question of two cultures?" (in part III of this volume), the presence or absence of an EHEA-style qualifications framework is not a relevant factor to the substantial difference issue.

Some best practice considerations

In the light of these developments, the extant Lisbon Recognition Convention and its subsidiary texts, and empirical evidence of how competent recognition authorities approach the question of substantial difference in their work, how might European Region and EHEA recognition authorities consider good practices that preserve the integrity of their national systems, while being responsive to the realities of global diversity? How can the issue of substantial difference be limited to those instances where there are substantive rather than procedural, habitual or cultural considerations that may force the rejection, or partial recognition, of a qualification? Below is a table of possible suggestions.

Good practices	Less accepted/unacceptable practices
Adhering to the spirit as well as the letter of the Lisbon Recognition Convention and subsidiary texts.	Narrowly interpreting the convention and subsidiary texts to protect restrictive practices.

Good practices	Less accepted/unacceptable practices
Avoiding reliance on national or systemic biases, such as assuming that qualifications or credits from country X are always suspect or inferior, and basing decisions on defensible criteria.	Allowing national prejudices, political considerations or unsubstantiated impressions to influence recognition decisions.
Ensuring that competent national quality assurance agencies are fully recognised in systems where these exist, and especially in countries belonging to the European Region and adhering to the principles of the UNESCO recognition conventions.	Policies or practices that selectively exclude competent national quality assurance agencies in some countries from recognition but not others, even if these agencies are properly recognised in the home country and there is no evidence of fraud or corruption.
Providing transparent information, in English as well as the national language, about recognition requirements, policies and procedures.	Providing only summary information in widely spoken languages and restricting access to detailed and fully transparent information about requirements, policies and procedures.
Ensuring that information about the competent recognition authority(ies) is(are) made available widely, including by other agencies (such as embassies), educational institutions and organisations.	Providing inadequate information about the existence and services of competent recognition authorities, or restricting access to them.
Providing information and electronic links, where possible, to other relevant national competent recognition authorities in professional and vocational fields.	Forcing applicants for recognition, or their sponsors, to search for the correct competent recognition authority in a particular field if it is not the ENIC/NARIC or the Ministry of Education.
Ensuring that applicants are advised about required information, that decisions are taken in a timely manner, and that routes of appeal are available and communicated to applicants.	Forcing applicants to guess about required information and deadlines; having passive bureaucratic attitudes or excessively long decision times; and failing to have or communicate information about appeals.
Not requiring impossible or unfair prerequisites from applicants, such as prior possession of a work permit or visa (for which recognition is itself a prerequisite) or demanding proof of citizenship or a residency permit.	Refusing to deal with recognition applicants who do not already possess work permits, visas, citizenship or resident status, or making the procedures for them difficult or impossible to reasonably comply with.

Good practices	Less accepted/unacceptable practices
Making sure that specific directives internal to the EU or EHEA are not unfairly imposed on recognition applicants from outside.	Imposing internal European directive requirements on external applicants when this is not called for by the purpose for which recognition is sought.
Ensuring that applicants for recognition from countries inside the EU or EHEA are compliant with applicable regional directives and policies.	Ignoring or making excessive exceptions to EU or EHEA directives and policies for recognition applicants from within the EU or EHEA.
Emphasising the function of qualifications and the purpose for which recognition is sought in making recognition decisions, and avoiding, insofar as possible, legalistic or formulaic procedures involving detailed determinations of exact equivalence.	Relying upon narrow, unduly conservative and detailed equivalence or nostrification procedures that do not take into account learning outcomes or the purpose for which recognition is sought, or the natural diversity within and across systems.
Working to ensure that all competent recognition authorities and guidelines, including those for regulated occupations, take into account the global dimension and the need to permit mobility as well as the principles outlined in the Lisbon Recognition Convention and its subsidiary texts.	Making no effort to educate other competent recognition authorities, agency leadership or professional bodies about modern principles of recognition, or the need to provide competent recognition authorities adequate discretion to deal with academic or professional mobility cases.
If the level, content, or focus of a qualification or its issuing institution is in question, making sure that it is evaluated in terms of its function and the purpose for which recognition is sought, and whether the applicant satisfies the competences expected in the host country.	Passively relying on legalistic fidelity to institutional or programme type, title or focus or to the policies of the home system, irrespective of other evidence such as competences, agreements or the purpose for which recognition is sought.
Relying on accreditation or quality assurance by a recognised national authority, where this exists, as good evidence of an institution's or programme's legitimacy.	Ignoring evidence of quality assurance by properly recognised national authorities, selectively manipulating such evidence or demanding that the quality assurance be European or domestic, even if the institution or programme belongs to an external system.

Good practices	Less accepted/unacceptable practices
No distinction is made between qualifications or periods of study earned at private versus public institutions, so long as the private institution is properly recognised by the competent quality assurance authorities in the system under which the credits or qualification was issued.	Periods of study and qualifications completed at private institutions are considered substantially different from those completed at public institutions, and are treated negatively, without regard to other factors or to the recognised status of the private provider in its home system.
Providing fair and transparent consideration of qualifications and credits from distance learning providers so long as these are properly accredited or otherwise quality-assured in their home system and there is no evidence of fraud.	Refusing to recognise, or showing unwarranted bias against, distance learning even when it is properly quality-assured by national competent authorities and there is no evidence of any suspicion of fraud.
Providing fair and transparent consideration of qualifications and credits from transnational providers so long as these are properly quality-assured in the home system, are permitted to operate in the host country, and can be shown to follow the principles outlined in the Code of Good Practice for the Provision of Transnational Education.	Refusing to recognise, or showing unwarranted bias against transnational providers even if they can be shown to be properly accredited in their home system, permitted to operate as educational institutions by the host country, and can be shown to comply with the Code of Good Practice in the Provision of Transnational Education.
In the case of non-recognised providers, using the typology contained in "Qualifications from non-recognized institutions: an overview of the issue" to determine whether the provider is in fact legitimate and whether the resulting qualification may deserve a partial or fully positive recognition decision.	Automatically rejecting all qualifications from non-recognised institutions, including religious seminaries, government or military institutions, health care training facilities, adult education centres and pre-Bologna systems notwithstanding the fact that these may sometimes be legitimate and comparable to recognised qualifications.
Refusing to recognise any qualifications or credits from known bogus providers or institutions accredited by bogus accrediting agencies, and working to educate recognition applicants as well as to work with appropriate enforcement agencies to combat educational fraud.	Laxity in being alert to the possibility of educational fraud, or permitting applicants possessing bogus qualifications to study and work in one's country.

Good practices	Less accepted/unacceptable practices
Ensuring that legitimate core requirements pertaining to the purpose for which recognition is sought are met; if necessary, offering advice to applicants presenting different qualifications and providing partial recognition where possible.	Being too liberal or conservative with regard to relevant core requirements pertaining to the purpose for which recognition is sought, or using excessively legalistic criteria that may inadvertently allow persons lacking in necessary competences to attempt studying or working, or result in rejecting fully or partially qualified applicants.
Non-academic elements of a qualification are considered to be relevant only if they pertain to the purpose for which recognition is sought and are legitimate core expectations of the host country, such as when experience, internships or practicums are required in order to have adequate professional preparation, they may be ignored if they are irrelevant to the purpose for which recognition is sought.	Non-academic elements of a qualification are always treated negatively, even if they have nothing to do with the qualification itself or purpose for which recognition is sought, and the applicant has otherwise satisfied all legitimate core requirements for recognition. When relevant to the purpose for which recognition is sought, they are not taken into account or treated negatively.
If a substantial difference is shown to exist, the competent recognition authority weighs this fact together with other evidence to determine if it is relevant to the purpose for which recognition is sought, whether it is an unavoidable obstacle to full recognition or can be ignored due to other factors, and if it cannot be ignored whether partial recognition can be offered.	If a substantial difference is shown to exist, the competent recognition authority immediately rejects the application even if the issue does not pertain to the purpose for which recognition is sought, or there are other mitigating factors, and does not consider offering even partial recognition.
Periods of study should be given the same fair consideration as are completed qualifications, and studies abroad en route to a qualification are not considered a substantial difference issue, whether or not the period of study was part of an organised programme or was undertaken by the student independently, unless there are legitimate quality reservations about the study period or the institution where it was undertaken.	Periods of study abroad are regarded negatively and are ignored or counted against the credits and other requirements necessary for a recognised qualification in the national system, even if they are legitimate and were undertaken at a recognised institution.

The above list is not exhaustive, but it is based on the findings of the Working Party on Substantial Differences and the research conducted to discover information about how the concept is interpreted and used in real life. The concept of substantial differences is presented in the Lisbon Recognition Convention but is not defined in detail. So it has been left to the ENICs and NARICs to determine its full operational meaning and to evolve acceptable approaches for considering whether a substantial difference exists and what to do in cases where it does. This effort has been intimately linked to the process of implementing the Lisbon Recognition Convention. Under the terms of the convention, evidence of a substantial difference between a host country expectation, with respect to a qualification or period of study and what is presented by an applicant for recognition, is the primary legitimate basis for denying recognition or granting only partial recognition. As a consequence, the issue of substantial difference looms large in recognition decision making and permeates nearly every aspect of the recognition process. It should not come as a surprise that the complexity of the issues surrounding substantial difference mirror the complexity of recognition in general.

What has been learned from the formal study of substantial differences is that competent recognition authorities have, by and large, successfully addressed this issue and are using the concept judiciously. The situation is not perfect and there remain areas of controversy. In particular, the matter of the recognition of professional qualifications is still fraught with narrow legal requirements that are relatively inflexible, especially if the purpose for which recognition is sought is eligibility to become licensed and work, rather than to continue academic studies in the professional field. But other potential areas of controversy – such as length, credits, focus, titles and content questions – appear no longer to pose a threat to fair recognition outside the professional area. What remains to be tackled are what one might call residual problems. These include:

– the relative conservatism and legalism of some competent recognition authorities as compared to others, which could result in inconsistent treatment of similar issues and – over time – adversely affect the attractiveness of some countries and international mobility;

– lingering prejudices in some countries, occasionally reflected in formal policies, about the general quality of some systems in the European Region (and elsewhere) or the quality assurance in such systems, which are not based on objective evidence so much as on historical attitudes, politics, neo-imperialism or ignorance;

– some continuing resistance to the legitimacy of even properly regulated private, distance or transnational education, despite the fact that nearly all countries legally permit these options to exist and that they are explicitly recognised by EU, EHEA and UNESCO instruments;

– technical questions related to the proper way to deal with legitimate non-recognised institutions, adult or lifelong learning, non-credit qualifications, and differences in how countries define levels and types of education where the learning outcomes and purpose are similar, even though the status of the issuing institutions differs;

– the continuing challenges of obtaining, providing and sharing reliable information both among competent recognition authorities and to the stakeholders (licensing boards, immigration authorities, employers, unions and associations, academic institutions, government officials and agencies) and the citizens who rely on it.

These remaining challenges are important. Recognition is a continuously evolving process, and there will no doubt be new challenges emerging in the years to come, just as there remain residual problems resulting from the fact that old habits often die hard, and national systems vary in the speed and degree with which change is possible. This process must be respected because genuine substantial difference issues continue to exist and countries naturally vary in the ways in which their educational systems respond to issues of recognition. If the evidence indicates that excessively legalistic approaches are not a good way to approach substantial difference, one can also make a good argument that excessively flexible approaches are equally unsatisfactory. In the author's own country, the United States, for example, the existence of an almost completely unregulated recognition process has proved no better at achieving fairness and consistency than excessively narrow regulation has done elsewhere. The trick, and the challenge, is to achieve a balance that best preserves the rights of applicants for recognition to fair, transparent and timely service; the interests of employers, academic institutions and professions in ensuring that admissions, hiring and licensing standards are maintained in ways that preserve their institutional integrity; and the interest of governments in ensuring the common good and public safety. Good recognition principles and practices point the way. But reaching the goal is a constantly evolving process that requires the dedication of each professional and stakeholder.

An agenda for further development

Sjur Bergan

A quick look back

In terms of recognition policies, the 1990s were markedly different from the first decade of the 21st century in several ways. The 1990s was a decade in which the framework of Europe changed profoundly, as witnessed by the membership of the Council of Europe. In 1989, the Council of Europe had 23 member states, by the end of 1995 it had 38, by the end of 1999 it had 41 and as of 2009 it has 47. This growth in membership is rooted in the political changes that took place in Europe around 1990 and that made co-operation between the eastern and western part of the continent much easier than before. The UNESCO Europe Region changed much less in formal composition, since the countries of central and eastern Europe were members before the democratic changes of the late 1980s and early 1990s. However, the UNESCO framework was also enlarged by countries that became independent in the course of the decade in Europe, and co-operation within the region – which includes Canada, Israel and the United States as well as some of the newly independent countries of Central Asia in addition to geographical Europe – became much easier. The European Union has also expanded greatly in membership both in the 1990s and the 2000s.

The extended membership of all regional organisations and the vast changes in educational systems meant that the picture of education across Europe and the European Region was more diverse than it had previously been. This was due in part to greater diversity among the co-operating countries – more members meant more differences – but it was also due to developments within countries. Whereas many countries had long had a unitary system of traditional, publicly run universities, national systems were increasingly diversified. And these systems underwent reforms that blurred historical distinctions among types, and even levels, of education within the national system. For example, in the United Kingdom and in Germany, the traditional divide between polytechnics and *Fachhochschulen* respectively, and universities, were bridged by laws making the UK polytechnics universities with all rights and privileges, and by making German *Fachhochschulen* "universities of applied sciences", able to offer all university degrees except the research doctorate. Other countries that had traditionally had a unitary system of traditional universities developed a binary system, by establishing a set of more specialised institutions, offering more professionally oriented programmes. However, in many of these countries, the distinction between the two parts of the system was less than clear-cut.

In many countries, public higher education was supplemented by private institutions and programmes, and especially from the late 1990s onwards, traditional on-site education was supplemented by new forms of provision: offshore, online distance learning, transnational and others. While the new forms of provision carried many names, some common elements were that old typologies were modified, the issue of control ceased to be a state monopoly, and face to face interaction between teachers and students was supplemented, or even replaced, by other forms of interaction in both traditional and distance providers. None of these changes were absolute. Some countries had developed *Fachhochschule* types of institutions before the 1990s; private provision was a strong element in some countries, notably – but not exclusively – in North America, and the traditional lecture had long since ceased to be the only form of interaction between students and teachers. However, the pace of change quickened and both the perception and reality of increasing diversification between and within the education system was strongly felt.

At the same time, the international legal framework for the recognition of qualifications and institutions had been relatively static. In the European Region, this framework comprised five Council of Europe conventions, four of which dated from the 1950s and early 1960s, and one regional UNESCO convention dating from 1979 (Bergan and Rauhvargers, 2005). It seemed clear that this complex legal framework needed to be updated and the Council of Europe and UNESCO together concluded that the best alternative was to develop a new convention to replace all previous conventions. This proposition was accepted by member states, and work was started on the Lisbon Recognition Convention, which was adopted in 1997.

In recognition terms, the 1990s were therefore a decade in which there was serious discussion about key recognition issues, and in which this discussion aimed at overhauling the international legal framework. The European Region was a pioneer in this sense, and it benefited from the fact that the European Region spans more broadly than geographical Europe with the participation of non-European countries like Canada, Israel and the United States as well as from the changed participation of the countries of central and eastern Europe.

From legal texts to good practice

The Lisbon Recognition Convention was a major achievement. It recast the legal framework for recognition in the European Region and it attracted interest from other parts of the world. For some years, the focus of the work of the Council of Europe and UNESCO in this area shifted from developing a legal framework to encouraging adherence to it. The Lisbon Recognition Convention came into force with the fifth ratification in early 1999 and the number of ratifications grew rapidly – in fact, unusually rapidly for an international treaty. As of August 2009, 49 states had ratified the convention and a further four had signed it and were in the process of ratification.

At the same time, the Council of Europe and UNESCO, as well as member states, were acutely aware that even if the Lisbon Recognition Convention was a solid achievement and a much needed revision of the international legal framework, a legal text is only as good as its implementation. Around 2000, emphasis therefore shifted from developing the legal framework to putting it into practice. If the 1990s were, in a sense, a decade of developing legislation, the 2000s became a decade of developing good practice in order to make the legislation a reality.

This shift in focus coincided with some further international trends in higher education. In Europe, the Bologna Process took shape in 1999, inspired by the large ministerial meeting in Bologna in 1999, as well as by the meeting of four ministers – from France, Germany, Italy and the United Kingdom – at the Sorbonne in 1998. The Bologna Process was a European process, first limited to countries with a formal relationship to given European Union programmes and from 2003 open to all states party to the European Cultural Convention who committed to the goals of the process, but it was in many ways a reaction to developments not only in Europe but also globally. Not least, some of the key policies of the Bologna Process drew stronger inspiration from North America than many European policy makers were prepared to admit. The reform of the degree structure towards a three tier structure of bachelor, master and doctorate, later followed by the development of an overarching qualifications framework for the EHEA, is one important example with strong implications for recognition policy and practice, as explored elsewhere in this book.

Worldwide, the increasing diversification of higher education provision, including the rapid development of non-traditional provision, gave rise to greater concern for quality assurance. Whereas in Europe it had traditionally broadly been assumed that public provision was by definition of adequate quality, the increasing diversification brought not only a concern about the quality of private provision but also the realisation that traditional assumptions about the quality of public provision did not quite stand up to scrutiny. Of course, in some countries, quality assurance or accreditation had been a part of public higher education policy for some time, notably in the United States and in Europe – the United Kingdom was a pioneer in this area. The change in attitudes can be illustrated by the discussions around the Lisbon Recognition Convention. In 1996-97, there was still debate about whether a formal system of external quality assurance was needed or not, and Section VIII of the convention includes provisions for countries that have such a system, as well as for those who do not. Only five years later, the discussion was no longer about whether such a system was needed but what kind of system was desirable. Today, it is difficult to see how a party to the convention could fulfil its obligations under Section VIII without making reference to the outcomes of its external quality assurance exercise.

Challenges ahead

The world of sports has an attractive slogan – "a sound mind in a sound body". If we were to coin a similar slogan for the world of recognition, it might perhaps be something along the lines of "sound practice based on a sound legal framework". Without commenting on whether the world of sports lives up to its slogan – even if numerous cases of drug taking could give rise to some doubts – we have to admit that the world of recognition is not one of universally good practice.

Again, the EHEA provides an example. In 2007, ministers submitted what they called "national action plans for recognition", responding to their own commitment made in 2005 and following guidelines developed by the ENIC and NARIC networks and adopted by the Bologna Follow-Up Group. The results were less than encouraging (Rauhvargers and Rusakova, forthcoming). To start with, many of the action plans were in fact reports on the current state of affairs, with few indications of what the countries in question intended to do to improve their current practice. Whether a description of practice or planned developments, however, the plans showed a broad range of practices –ranging from progressive practice aiming to assist individual learners while making sure that sufficient quality was ensured, to far too many examples of rigid, legalistic practice. The national action plans amply demonstrated the existence of "two cultures" of recognition (Bergan, in Part III of this volume). Less than ideal practices were referred to in all the categories covered by the survey, ranging from legal provision, through recognition practice and information provision, to the structures of the national information centres and their co-operation – or not – with the agencies responsible for quality assurance. Examples of practice where there is considerable scope for improvement include such diverse examples as applying different recognition procedures to different kinds of degrees, using programme duration and content details as the main criteria for recognition, requiring that applicants present all documents in official (and hence expensive) translation into the language of the country in which recognition is sought, even if the original documents are in widely understood foreign languages, attempting to review the foreign higher education institution, department and programme instead of checking the quality assurance status with the issuing country's quality assurance body and refusing recognition when a relevant qualification to compare the foreign qualification to cannot be found in the higher education system of the host country. And these are mere examples; the full list is considerably longer and even that list is probably not exhaustive.

The greatest overall challenge is moving the world of recognition more solidly from a legalistic culture to one offering services to learners, while ensuring that recognition is not granted when it cannot be justified. In that context, perhaps one of the most egregious examples of legalistic mindset was the reported example of one competent recognition authority which thought its public service obligation was satisfied by posting its rules and procedures on the office bulletin board, which of course was inside a difficult-to-locate government building with restricted public access. This sort of thing is not worthy of the spirit of recognition, nor is it worthy of the commitment of Europe or its global partners to transparency, access and the social dimension.

The main challenge, then, is to develop attitudes. The ENIC and NARIC networks have started to do so through the Working Party on Substantial Differences and through the work described in parts of this book, most notably the analysis of concrete cases. Such analysis is invaluable, because it obliges credentials evaluators to state their reasons for reaching a given verdict on a specific qualification. Hence, their reasons are open to questions and challenges from others, as well as from themselves. One good example is shown in Bas Wegewijs' article in this volume, where many credentials evaluators stated that they would have preferred to seek less legalistic solutions than they are currently able to do in their own national context. In two consecutive years, "simulation exercises" of this kind were the main item on the agenda of the annual network meetings, and even if there were no formal conclusions, there was open and free discussion and hopefully an opening of minds and a questioning of one's own practice. It was important that, in most cases, the examples were fictitious, so that no members of the networks were put in the uncomfortable position of having to defend their own national practice, even if they might themselves have started to question certain aspects of it.

The ENIC and NARIC networks are the most important arenas for the development of recognition practice in the European Region, but they are not the only ones. Members of the ENIC and NARIC networks must launch similar debates in their own countries. Even if the ENICs and NARICs are important resource centres in their own national contexts, most applications for recognition are decided at higher education institutions, in professional or other bodies, or by employers. ENICs and NARICs should initiate work at national level on how credentials evaluators at institutions, in professional bodies and elsewhere interpret the concept of substantial differences and how this is reflected in their practical work. Workshops at national level on substantial differences, along the lines of those held at the 2007 and 2008 ENIC and NARIC meetings, would be of great value. At European level, the European Association for International Education (EAIE)[55] is an important forum for higher education administrators, with a special professional section for admissions officers and credentials evaluators (ACE)[56] in which many ENIC and NARIC representatives are active. In North America, the Association of International Educators (NAFSA)[57] and the American Association of Collegiate Registrars and Admissions Officers (AACRAO)[58] play similar roles and served as models for the EAIE in its early years. These and other international or regional forums, where credentials evaluators meet, could play an important role in developing reflection, discourse and practice around the concept of substantial differences.

Making contact with employers is a particular challenge. Large companies that hire internationally are generally well aware of different qualifications and education systems, but small and medium size employers, or those who operate mainly domestically, are not. Nevertheless, with increasing migration, it is unlikely that they will never be faced with a foreign qualification. Whether employers take a broad or narrow view of substantial differences – even if they are unlikely to express

---

55. www.eaie.org/.
56. www.eaie.org/ACE/.
57. www.nafsa.org/.
58. www.aacrao.org/.

their views in those terms – may ultimately decide whether those with foreign qualifications are integrated into the labour market or not. ENICs and NARICs, as well as higher education institutions and public authorities, have much work to do to establish proper relations with employers and their organisations in this area.

Whereas governments are often thought of as unitary actors, they in fact consist of ministries and agencies with specific mandates. Even when political co-ordination at the top works well – and there are examples to the contrary – ministries and agencies also look to their specific remits and may well look at the same issue from different angles. Even if in the views of educators, foreign qualifications are an educational issue, immigration authorities are likely to see them as an issue of migration and labour authorities as an employment issue. Without resorting to Plato's images of prisoners in a cave seeing the world only as shadows, or of the blind defining an elephant according to the part of the animal they are able to touch, so that they believe an elephant is as soft as its hide or as hard as its tusks, it must be recognised that different concerns, all of which may not only be legitimate but specific parts of overall government policy, may lead to different and even contradictory decisions in individual cases. ENICs and NARICs should therefore engage with other public authorities, and in particular with those responsible for areas like immigration and labour policy or licensing boards. Such contact should not be limited to individual cases, which are likely to be problematic and require rapid decisions, but should extend to developing a better understanding of the underlying principles, so that some of the individual cases may be prevented from developing into problems. One example is that credentials evaluators will often be able to assess the real qualifications of people even if they lack complete documentation, as may often be the case with refugees or others who for valid reasons are reluctant or unable to make contact with the authorities of their home countries.

Reflection on substantial differences should not be limited to admissions officers and credentials evaluators, however. Higher education policy makers, whether institutional leaders or in public authorities, set – or should set – the tone for the debate. They develop the regulations that credentials evaluators follow, they set the general tone of public discourse on higher education and they can help create a climate of open reflection – or the opposite. If leading policy makers signal that a country's practice and system should be defended at all costs and that questioning its practices could be detrimental to its international esteem, it is difficult for individual credentials evaluators to be inquisitive. If, on the other hand, leading policy makers recognise that what is already good can be made even better by constantly questioning and seeking to improve one's practice, and if they underline that the purpose of public policy is to help individual learners as well as to develop the overall quality of the system, this would most likely encourage creativity among credentials evaluators. Helping individuals is not necessarily opposed to furthering quality, yet our discourse often gives the illusion that it is.

Quality is not something that is furthered by decreasing numbers: a qualification is not of higher quality the fewer people hold it. Rather, high quality education is fit for purposes – and the plural is intentional. Public policies for higher education must recognise and reflect the multiple purposes of higher education. The current public discourse, at least in Europe, which strongly emphasises the economic function of higher education and devotes little thought to other purposes, such as preparation for citizenship, personal development and the development of a broad and advanced knowledge base, might itself contribute to the illusion that quality is one dimensional.

Ultimately, the challenge may be how our societies view diversity. We live in the proverbial "globalised world" (which begs the obvious question; what is a "non-globalised world?"), but the threats are often emphasised much more than the opportunities. Both are real, but the goal must be to enhance the opportunities and diminish the threats, something that is not done by longing for homogenous societies in which "equal" and "alike" are one and the same. Modern societies cannot function unless they are proficient in intercultural dialogue (Council of Europe, 2008).

While the principle that cultural diversity enriches our societies and that intercultural dialogue is needed is well accepted in official discourse as well as – in many cases – in private, practice is often different. We do not need to think of extremist fringes to find examples in which society at large seeks to mould rather than let blossom. Again, examples from linguistic practice are illustrative. Knowledge of foreign languages is often considered as proof of being educated and broad-minded (even if the two are, alas, not necessarily one and the same). Yet, in daily practice, whether officially or privately, we often seek to make foreign names and sounds fit into our preconceived models. Respecting someone's name is respecting their culture and their dignity, yet many insist on turning København into Copenhagen (English), on Valencia into Valence (French), thereby providing ample opportunity for mixing up cities in France and Spain that respecting the original version of the names would have avoided, or to undertake a similar exercise by turning München into Monaco (Italian). Close to Oslo, there is a place called Østerås, which means "eastern hill". Take away the diacritical mark on the ø, so that you have Osterås, and you have "cheese hill" instead. What you have if you take away the diacritical mark on the å is left to the reader's imagination. We must perhaps be happy that, so far, there have been few attempts to turn Rio de Janeiro into January River!

Personal names fare no better. The world's most famous soldier is Czech and goes by the name of Švejk in his home country, but only rarely outside it. Internationally, he is Sveik, Svejk, Sveijk, Schweik, Schwaik, or several other variations. A reference article that turned up prominently when Googling the name of his creator, Jaroslav Hašek, even uses two versions of the good soldier's name in two successive paragraphs. A friend of this author, who admits to having a name that is uncommon even in her home country, has registered 22 versions used in international documents referring to her and is still counting. And several languages, including English, French and Spanish, have several accepted standards used in different countries, yet users of one are not always tolerant of other varieties, all the while deploring how minor linguistic differences have been used in much more fundamental disputes in other places in Europe or elsewhere.

Recognising foreign qualifications for their real worth implies curbing our tendency as human beings to accentuate differences, at least when this is to our advantage. We can all think of what makes us different from our neighbours, but we are perhaps less prompt to consider whether these differences are really significant, or whether they rather give us a richer and more colourful experience. A specific area of higher education policy may perhaps serve as an illustration. While institutions have been ranked explicitly or unconsciously for quite some time, the past few years have seen a strong development towards systematic national or international rankings of institutions. Rankings give rise to a number of questions, including whether their methodology is indeed sound and whether they give any reliable information on institutions as such, rather than on specific parts of their activities, such as research in natural science or medicine. In our context, however, the two most important questions are perhaps whether – even if we could assume that the methodology of ranking were sound – deciding if an institution's ranking as number 25 or 35 is indeed meaningful in the context of recognition. In our terminology, is such a difference indeed substantial? The answer of the recognition community is clear; rankings are not to be used to indicate any difference in quality between institutions and qualifications in terms of recognition. The second issue is, however, whether the strong focus on ranking will not, over time, also encourage credentials evaluators to look more for possible differences than for possible similarities between qualifications. This would profoundly change what should be the starting point in assessing foreign qualifications. It could change the approach from looking for good reasons to recognise, to looking for possible reasons to refuse recognition. This author agrees with those who maintain that institutional rankings are probably here to stay, but he disagrees with the unstated implication of this statement: that public authorities must relate to rankings and even use them in their policies. There is, in this author's view, little in the current state of affairs to support such a dedication and much that speaks against it.

Recognition beyond technicalities

The recognition of qualifications is often thought of as an eminently technical occupation, perhaps best conducted in obscure offices in the far corners of campuses or ministries. Yet developments over the past couple of decades, including but not limited to the Bologna Process, have brought recognition policies and practices to the very core of higher education policy. As the considerations of the importance of recognising diversity have highlighted, diversity is part of our daily lives and not recognising its value when it comes to qualifications is not only technically, but also morally, questionable. Individuals have a right to fair recognition of their qualifications (Lisbon Recognition Convention, Section III), and public authorities, policy makers and credentials evaluators have a duty to ensure this right. This does not, of course, mean that "anything goes", or that all qualifications must be recognised regardless of their merits. It does, however, mean that the merits of all qualifications must be recognised for what they are worth. Sometimes the conclusion will justifiably be that a qualification cannot be recognised, or that it can only be partially recognised, but the starting assumption should be that credentials evaluators should seek to identify how a foreign qualification may be recognised in their own system or qualifications framework; not that the foreign qualification should probably not be recognised.

Perhaps the need to respect and value diversity, which is the underlying principle of recognition, can be illustrated by another linguistic point. English distinguishes between the concepts of "equal" and "alike" or "similar" in a way that a number of other languages do not, and it is of course more difficult to make this distinction mentally and in practice if one's linguistic toolset does not encourage the distinction. In this author's native language, Norwegian, the linguistic distinction does exist: "alike" or "similar" is rendered as *lik(e)*,[59] whereas "equal" is rendered as *likeverdig(e)* (literally "of equal dignity"). *Likeverdig* is, however, considered a somewhat more literary or "elevated" form, so that in everyday speech the distinction is often not made. In everyday language, the statement that "all persons are equal" is often turned into "all persons are alike". By analogy, analysis of the national action plans referred to above demonstrates that the belief that to be equal, qualifications must be not only similar but almost alike, is alive and well in many countries. However, that statement may be inadequate: while referring to national recognition cultures is a convenient shortcut, and while it may not be entirely without foundation, credentials evaluators are individuals who, even if they are influenced by their environment and restrained by institutional practice and national regulations, have their own sets of attitudes, experience and practice. At the risk of oversimplification, one can find progressive credentials evaluators in countries with a generally legalistic recognition culture and vice versa. What we need to strive for in the years to come is developing a higher understanding, including in recognition, so that it becomes more widely accepted that two different qualifications may be *likeverdige* even if they are not *like*.

Much has been accomplished over the past couple of decades, and this author firmly believes that recognition practice today is more open-minded and less legalistic than it was 20 or 30 years ago. That is positive, but it is not enough. For recognition to be an area of policy and practice that seeks to find practical solutions to help individual holders of qualifications, policies and practice must continue to develop. We need legislation, but we also need legislation to be applied with a solid dose of common sense.

Throughout this book, we hope to have identified issues for further discussion and we hope to have stimulated further reflection as well as material for credentials evaluators, policy makers and others to reassess their own attitudes and practice. We are, however, painfully aware that a book, like a convention, is only an instrument.

---

59. The *–e* denotes the plural; there is no gender distinction in adjectives even if there is in nouns.

Practice is developed by people, and it is up to policy makers and practitioners to make recognition into an instrument that opens up possibilities, rather than one that closes opportunities. This book has hopefully provided some keys, but keys must be turned to open doors.

References

Bergan, S. and Rauhvargers, A. (eds), *Standards for recognition: the Lisbon Recognition Convention and its subsidiary texts*, Council of Europe Higher Education Series No. 3, Council of Europe Publishing, Strasbourg, 2005.

Council of Europe, *White Paper on Intercultural Dialogue "Living Together as Equals in Dignity"*, Strasbourg, 2008. Also available online at www.coe.int/t/dg4/intercultural/Source/White%20Paper_final_revised_EN.pdf.

Rauhvargers, A. and Rusakova, A., *Improving recognition in the European Higher Education Area: an analysis of national action plans*, Council of Europe Higher Education Series No. 12, Council of Europe Publishing (forthcoming).

List of authors

Editors

Sjur Bergan is Head of the Council of Europe's Department of Higher Education and History Teaching and was Co-Secretary of the ENIC Network until 2007. He is a member of the Bologna Follow-Up Group and chairs the Bologna Co-ordination Group on Qualifications Frameworks. Sjur Bergan is the author of *Qualifications: Introduction to a Concept*, the editor of several books in the Council of Europe Higher Education Series and the author of numerous articles on higher education policy.

E. Stephen Hunt is President of the ENIC Network and Head of the American ENIC. He chaired the ENIC Network's Working Party on Substantial Differences and is a frequent contributor of articles and presentations on the Bologna Process and transatlantic educational reform, as well as the author of several research monographs, including the American *Classification of Instructional Programs (CIP)*. E. Stephen Hunt served as Vice President of the ENIC Network in 2007-08 and was an advisory member of the team that negotiated the Lisbon Recognition Convention on behalf of the United States in 1996-97.

Contributors

Yves E. Beaudin is Head of the Canadian ENIC and was president of the ENIC Network in 2005-07. He was a member of the Working Party on Substantial Differences.

Carita Blomqvist is the Head of the Finnish ENIC/NARIC and the President of the Lisbon Recognition Convention Committee.

Lucie de Bruin is the Head of the Dutch ENIC/NARIC.

Rolf Lofstad is a credentials evaluator with the Norwegian ENIC/NARIC and a former member of the Lisbon Recognition Convention Committee, the NARIC Advisory Board and the Working Party on Substantial Differences.

Erwin Malfroy is the Head of the ENIC/NARIC of the Flemish Community of Belgium and a former member of the NARIC Advisory Board. He was a member of the Working Party on Substantial Differences.

Françoise Profit is Head of the French ENIC/NARIC and was President of the ENIC Network in 2007-09.

Jean-Philippe Restoueix is an administrator in the Council of Europe's Higher Education and Research Division and Co-Secretary of the ENIC Network.

Bas Wegewijs is a credentials evaluator with the Dutch ENIC/NARIC.

Peter J. Wells is an official of UNESCO/CEPES in Bucharest and Co-Secretary of the ENIC Network. He was a member of the Working Party on Substantial Differences.

Sales agents for publications of the Council of Europe
Agents de vente des publications du Conseil de l'Europe

BELGIUM/BELGIQUE
La Librairie Européenne -
The European Bookshop
Rue de l'Orme, 1
BE-1040 BRUXELLES
Tel.: +32 (0)2 231 04 35
Fax: +32 (0)2 735 08 60
E-mail: order@libeurop.be
http://www.libeurop.be

Jean De Lannoy/DL Services
Avenue du Roi 202 Koningslaan
BE-1190 BRUXELLES
Tel.: +32 (0)2 538 43 08
Fax: +32 (0)2 538 08 41
E-mail: jean.de.lannoy@dl-servi.com
http://www.jean-de-lannoy.be

BOSNIA AND HERZEGOVINA/
BOSNIE-HERZÉGOVINE
Robert's Plus d.o.o.
Marka Maruliça 2/V
BA-71000, SARAJEVO
Tel.: + 387 33 640 818
Fax: + 387 33 640 818
E-mail: robertsplus@bih.net.ba

CANADA
Renouf Publishing Co. Ltd.
1-5369 Canotek Road
CA-OTTAWA, Ontario K1J 9J3
Tel.: +1 613 745 2665
Fax: +1 613 745 7660
Toll-Free Tel.: (866) 767-6766
E-mail: order.dept@renoufbooks.com
http://www.renoufbooks.com

CROATIA/CROATIE
Robert's Plus d.o.o.
Marasoviçeva 67
HR-21000, SPLIT
Tel.: + 385 21 315 800, 801, 802, 803
Fax: + 385 21 315 804
E-mail: robertsplus@robertsplus.hr

CZECH REPUBLIC/
RÉPUBLIQUE TCHÈQUE
Suweco CZ, s.r.o.
Klecakova 347
CZ-180 21 PRAHA 9
Tel.: +420 2 424 59 204
Fax: +420 2 848 21 646
E-mail: import@suweco.cz
http://www.suweco.cz

DENMARK/DANEMARK
GAD
Vimmelskaftet 32
DK-1161 KØBENHAVN K
Tel.: +45 77 66 60 00
Fax: +45 77 66 60 01
E-mail: gad@gad.dk
http://www.gad.dk

FINLAND/FINLANDE
Akateeminen Kirjakauppa
PO Box 128
Keskuskatu 1
FI-00100 HELSINKI
Tel.: +358 (0)9 121 4430
Fax: +358 (0)9 121 4242
E-mail: akatilaus@akateeminen.com
http://www.akateeminen.com

FRANCE
La Documentation française
(diffusion/distribution France entière)
124, rue Henri Barbusse
FR-93308 AUBERVILLIERS CEDEX
Tél.: +33 (0)1 40 15 70 00
Fax: +33 (0)1 40 15 68 00
E-mail: commande@ladocumentationfrancaise.fr
http://www.ladocumentationfrancaise.fr

Librairie Kléber
1 rue des Francs Bourgeois
FR-67000 STRASBOURG
Tel.: +33 (0)3 88 15 78 88
Fax: +33 (0)3 88 15 78 80
E-mail: librairie-kleber@coe.int
http://www.librairie-kleber.com

GERMANY/ALLEMAGNE
AUSTRIA/AUTRICHE
UNO Verlag GmbH
August-Bebel-Allee 6
DE-53175 BONN
Tel.: +49 (0)228 94 90 20
Fax: +49 (0)228 94 90 222
E-mail: bestellung@uno-verlag.de
http://www.uno-verlag.de

GREECE/GRÈCE
Librairie Kauffmann s.a.
Stadiou 28
GR-105 64 ATHINAI
Tel.: +30 210 32 55 321
Fax.: +30 210 32 30 320
E-mail: ord@otenet.gr
http://www.kauffmann.gr

HUNGARY/HONGRIE
Euro Info Service
Pannónia u. 58.
PF. 1039
HU-1136 BUDAPEST
Tel.: +36 1 329 2170
Fax: +36 1 349 2053
E-mail: euroinfo@euroinfo.hu
http://www.euroinfo.hu

ITALY/ITALIE
Licosa SpA
Via Duca di Calabria, 1/1
IT-50125 FIRENZE
Tel.: +39 0556 483215
Fax: +39 0556 41257
E-mail: licosa@licosa.com
http://www.licosa.com

MEXICO/MEXIQUE
Mundi-Prensa México, S.A. De C.V.
Río Pánuco, 141 Delegacíon Cuauhtémoc
MX-06500 MÉXICO, D.F.
Tel.: +52 (01)55 55 33 56 58
Fax: +52 (01)55 55 14 67 99
E-mail: mundiprensa@mundiprensa.com.mx
http://www.mundiprensa.com.mx

NETHERLANDS/PAYS-BAS
Roodveldt Import BV
Nieuwe Hemweg 50
NE-1013 CX AMSTERDAM
Tel.: + 31 20 622 8035
Fax.: + 31 20 625 5493
Website: www.publidis.org
Email: orders@publidis.org

NORWAY/NORVÈGE
Akademika
Postboks 84 Blindern
NO-0314 OSLO
Tel.: +47 2 218 8100
Fax: +47 2 218 8103
E-mail: support@akademika.no
http://www.akademika.no

POLAND/POLOGNE
Ars Polona JSC
25 Obroncow Street
PL-03-933 WARSZAWA
Tel.: +48 (0)22 509 86 00
Fax: +48 (0)22 509 86 10
E-mail: arspolona@arspolona.com.pl
http://www.arspolona.com.pl

PORTUGAL
Livraria Portugal
(Dias & Andrade, Lda.)
Rua do Carmo, 70
PT-1200-094 LISBOA
Tel.: +351 21 347 42 82 / 85
Fax: +351 21 347 02 64
E-mail: info@livrariaportugal.pt
http://www.livrariaportugal.pt

RUSSIAN FEDERATION/
FÉDÉRATION DE RUSSIE
Ves Mir
17b, Butlerova ul.
RU-101000 MOSCOW
Tel.: +7 495 739 0971
Fax: +7 495 739 0971
E-mail: orders@vesmirbooks.ru
http://www.vesmirbooks.ru

SPAIN/ESPAGNE
Mundi-Prensa Libros, s.a.
Castelló, 37
ES-28001 MADRID
Tel.: +34 914 36 37 00
Fax: +34 915 75 39 98
E-mail: libreria@mundiprensa.es
http://www.mundiprensa.com

SWITZERLAND/SUISSE
Planetis Sàrl
16 chemin des Pins
CH-1273 ARZIER
Tel.: +41 22 366 51 77
Fax: +41 22 366 51 78
E-mail: info@planetis.ch

UNITED KINGDOM/ROYAUME-UNI
The Stationery Office Ltd
PO Box 29
GB-NORWICH NR3 1GN
Tel.: +44 (0)870 600 5522
Fax: +44 (0)870 600 5533
E-mail: book.enquiries@tso.co.uk
http://www.tsoshop.co.uk

UNITED STATES and CANADA/
ÉTATS-UNIS et CANADA
Manhattan Publishing Co
2036 Albany Post Road
USA-10520 CROTON ON HUDSON, NY
Tel.: +1 914 271 5194
Fax: +1 914 271 5886
E-mail: coe@manhattanpublishing.coe
http://www.manhattanpublishing.com

Council of Europe Publishing/Editions du Conseil de l'Europe
FR-67075 STRASBOURG Cedex
Tel.: +33 (0)3 88 41 25 81 – Fax: +33 (0)3 88 41 39 10 – E-mail: publishing@coe.int – Website: http://book.coe.int